mini
Barcelona

The Essential **Visitors'** Guide

Barcelona mini Explorer
ISBN 13 – 978-9948-03-445-2
ISBN 10 – 9948-03-445-7

Copyright © Explorer Group Ltd 2007
All rights reserved.

All maps © Explorer Group Ltd 2007

Front cover photograph: Sagrada Familia – Victor Romero

Printed and bound by
Emirates Printing Press, Dubai, UAE

Explorer Publishing & Distribution
PO Box 34275, Dubai, United Arab Emirates
Phone (+971 4) 340 8805
Fax (+971 4) 340 8806
Email info@explorerpublishing.com
Web www.explorerpublishing.com

The *Barcelona Mini Explorer* is a pocket-sized parcel of essential information that will help you make the most of your trip to this glorious city. It covers sights, culture, history, activities and the best places for eating and drinking. It is written by Barcelona residents, and brought to you by the same team responsible for the *Barcelona Explorer: The Complete Residents' Guide*. If you want to know more about what we do, or tell us what we've missed, go to www.explorerpublishing.com.

The Barcelona Mini Explorer

Editorial Team: Matt Farquharson, Tracy Fitzgerald, Helen Spearman, Grace Carnay
Contributing Editor: Alice Ross
Designer: Jayde Fernandes
Authors: Alice Ross, Cass Chapman, Emma Buckle, Hannah Pennell, Jennifer Baljko, Jethro Soutar, Julius Purcell, Paul Cannon, Susanna Jacobs
Photographers: Victor Romero, Matt Farquharson

Contents

Essentials

¡Viva Barcelona!

This is one of the most diverse cities in Europe. From the market-life to the nightlife, football to festivals, Barcelona will not disappoint.

For a relatively small city, Barcelona packs quite a punch, combining the very best of Spain with a verve and swagger that's all its own. Boasting a sunny climate, a knockout collection of historic buildings, a distinctive regional cuisine, and a hip, vibrant cultural scene, it's easy to see how the Catalan capital has become one of Europe's most visited cities.

Much of the city's charm lies in its diversity. In Barcelona, it's possible to sunbathe on the beach in the morning, head to the atmospheric former fisherman's district of Barceloneta for lunch, do some window-shopping on the broad, elegant boulevards of Eixample in the afternoon, and then head to the warren-like streets of the Gothic quarter for drinking, dining and nightlife.

There are museums, galleries and cultural centres galore, but some of Barcelona's best bits can be appreciated simply by taking a walk. The city is justly famous for the unique, whimsical architecture of Antoni Gaudí and his contemporaries, but it also boasts a large and exceptionally well-preserved collection of ancient buildings, some of which date back to the Middle Ages, and a bold collection of contemporary buildings by a dream team of architects including Norman Foster, Jean Nouvel, Frank Gehry and Richard Rogers.

However, more than the sights and activities, what keeps visitors coming back to Barcelona time and again is the city's attitude. It's a relaxed, tolerant, creative kind of place where the lunches are long and the bars stay open into the early hours. It has a style of its own, simultaneously trendy and deeply individualistic, where independent boutiques, bars and restaurants beat the chain venues every time, and every local under the age of 40 seems to have a video art project, fusion band, organic cafe or handmade jewellery business.

Locals take great pride in their quality of life, which is perhaps best experienced by visitors in the variety and freshness of food, whether it be the huge range of seafood, the market-fresh meat, fruit and vegetables, hearty traditional Catalan food or the burgeoning local haute cuisine scene that's springing up as a result of local boy Ferran Adrià's ever-growing global fame.

It's almost impossible to sample everything that Barcelona has to offer in just one trip, and returning visitors will find it is constantly changing, becoming ever-more cosmopolitan, while retaining the flair and feeling that make it so special.

Donde Esta...?

Barcelona has good public transport and a logical grid layout through Eixample. The muddle of alleys in the Gothic quarter are trickier to navigate, but are best enjoyed by simply getting lost. The Maps chapter, or the *Barcelona Mini Map* (in bookshops across town) should be all you need to find your way around.

Barcelona Checklist

01 La Rambla

A walk along the kilometre-long boulevard that cuts through the Ciutat Vella is an essential part of any visit to Barcelona. Although touristy, it remains the spiritual centre of the city. Lined with street artists, flower stalls and animal sellers, it's a blur of action. See p.64.

02 Tibidabo

Getting to the church that perches high above Barcelona is just half of the fun: the journey includes a trip in a century-old tram and a funicular. At the summit is a quaint, picturesque funfair, and an exhilarating bird's-eye view across the city. See p.99.

03 Barceloneta Beach

It may be artificial, and crowded during summer, but how many cities can boast a beach this close to the city centre? It's a buzzing place to spend an afternoon, with a strip of bars and restaurants and great views of Frank Gehry's shimmering fish sculpture. See p.180.

04 Passeig de Gràcia

Even if you can't afford to shop in the high-fashion boutiques, there's plenty on Passeig de Gràcia for feasting the eyes. Aside from haute couture window displays, there are two Gaudí masterpieces, La Pedrera (p.92) and Casa Batlló (p.90).

05 Museu Picasso

A huge collection of the artist's early works and later masterpieces are housed in stunning buildings deep in the Born. The museum explains the artistic evolution of Barcelona's favourite adoptive son, and also stages excellent temporary exhibitions. See p.71.

06 Montjuïc

Even if you choose to bypass the art galleries, museums and other attractions that are scattered across the hill, Montjuïc offers an escape from the city and unbeatable views. There's enough here to fill up hours of very enjoyable wandering. See p.84.

07 La Boqueria

Barcelona's largest and most spectacular food market is an explosion of colours, noises and smells, with lively stalls, each specialising in fresh foods, seafood, nuts, spices or even just eggs. Pull up a stool at one of the bars at the back for the freshest tapas in town (p.140).

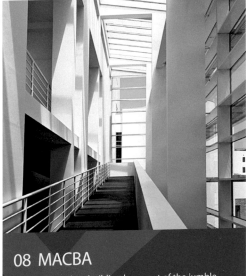

08 MACBA

This striking white building leaps out of the jumble of Raval streets. Inside is an uncompromising contemporary art museum, with temporary exhibitions that can be quite obscure, yet intriguingly cutting-edge. See p.75.

09 Els Quatre Gats

The sumptuous interiors and excellent food are only half the story: Els Quatre Gats was the hangout of choice for Barcelona's artistic elite, including Picasso, who did the menu design. Prices are high, but it's worth stopping in, if only for coffee. See p.167.

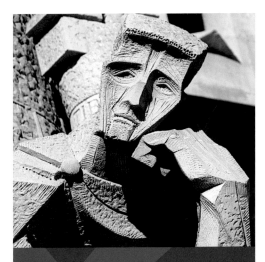

10 La Sagrada Familia

Antoni Gaudí's final project is still a work in progress: the exuberant, eccentric masterpiece continues to rise slowly from the Eixample. Its distinctive spires are among the city's defining symbols, and new additions to the building are bold and modern. See p.93.

For Families

Barcelona's technicolour charms are well-suited to small children, while parents will be relieved to find Catalan restaurateurs and hoteliers child-friendly. The aquarium (p.78) will keep kids occupied for hours, as will the nearby zoo (p.70). The wonderland atmosphere of Gaudí's Park Güell (p.98), with its tactile, multicoloured benches, is great for running off steam, while his Nativity Façade at the Sagrada Familia (p.93) is a riot of animal sculptures. The CosmoCaixa science museum (p.95) has a hands-on kids' zone and an impressive rainforest habitat, while in the evenings the sound and light show of the Magic Fountains at Plaça d'Espanya has a certain charm.

For Culture Vultures

There's enough classical music on offer in Barcelona to satisfy every taste: it joins forces with over-the-top architecture at Luís Domènech i Muntaner's Palau de la Música Catalana (p.71). The lavishly-refurbished Liceu opera house (p.210) stages some excellent productions, and the sleek lines of the modern Auditori (p.210) play host to more challenging orchestral pieces.

Art buffs will be happy too. Picasso, Miró and Catalan superstar Antoni Tàpies each have their own museums (p.10, 85 and 92 respectively), MNAC (p.86) has excellent early Catalan art, and more contemporary work is shown at Palau de la Virreina (p.66), CCCB (p.74), and MACBA (p.75).

For Sports Fans

Although the city boosted its sporting credentials by hosting the much-praised 1992 Olympics, it's better-known for being the home of the *azulgranas*: FCBarcelona. The impressive Camp Nou (p.98), Europe's largest stadium, with a capacity of 98,000, is also home to a football museum and offers visitors guided tours of the stadium. Watching a match is an incredible experience as it reveals the deep passion that the team inspires. Tickets can be bought from www.servicaixa. com. For a taste of the city's Olympic past, visit the Olympic ring (p.86) on Montjuïc, home to the Olympic Stadium, the Palau Sant Jordi arena and the Catalan Sports Institute. Here you'll find guided tours of the stadium and other facilities.

For Foodies

No trip to Barcelona is complete without a visit to the Boqueria market (p.140), one of the most colourful and lively places in the city. It's crucial to sample what they do with all that fresh food, so head to Kaiku for a lunchtime paella facing the sea (p.182), Jai-Ca for absurdly fresh, cheap tapas and a rowdy atmosphere (p.183), or Gaig (p.198) and El Racó d'en Freixa (p.204) to check out contemporary Catalan cuisine at its most outlandish. For more traditional Catalan food, try Can Culleretes (p.167) or Café de l'Acadèmia (p.166). For food from elsewhere in Spain, try La Bodegueta (p.199) for its old fashioned tapas, or Comerç 24 (p.175), for it's highly stylised Spanish cuisine.

Visiting Barcelona

Although Catalans have a reputation for being slightly abrupt, natives will show their warmth towards visitors who make a little effort.

Getting There

Barcelona International Airport (www.aena.es), known as El Prat, is 12 kilometres from the city, and is served by budget carriers and established airlines. E-tickets are accepted by most, but electronic check-in is only usually available on non-budget airlines.

Normal baggage allowances are 20kg of hold luggage and one piece to carry on, although some low-cost providers now charge a small fee for items in the hold. As in many other European countries, gels and liquids in containers over 150ml cannot be carried in hand luggage.

From The Airport

Take your pick from taxis, buses and trains. Taxi ranks are outside each terminal; expect to pay €20 to €25 to the city centre. Aerobus (www.sarfa.com, 93 415 60 20) runs to the city centre roughly every 10 minutes. Tickets, purchased on the bus, cost €3.90 one-way and it stops at key points between Plaça d'Espanya and Plaça de Catalunya (both of which have metro stations).

Public bus number 46 runs to Plaça d'Espanya, and night bus N17 stops near Plaça de Catalunya. Both cost €1.25;

Airlines

Aer Lingus	93 342 88 90	www.aerlingus.com
Air France	90 220 70 90	www.airfrance.com
British Airways	90 211 13 33	www.ba.com
Continental Airlines	90 096 12 66	www.continental.com
Delta Airlines	93 478 23 00	www.delta.com
easyJet	80 707 00 70	www.easyjet.com
Iberia	90 240 05 00	www.iberia.es
KLM Royal Dutch Airlines	90 222 27 47	www.klm.com
Lufthansa	90 222 01 01	www.lufthansa.com
Singapore Airlines	93 297 13 08	www.singaporeair.com
Spanair	93 298 33 62	www.spanair.com
Vueling Airlines	90 233 39 33	www.vueling.com

tickets can be used for zone one public transport transfers within 60 minutes.

The Renfe Cercanías train (www.renfe.es, 90 224 02 02) links the airport with the Sants and França railway stations and stops at Passeig de Gràcia. Tickets, which can also be used for zone one transfers, cost €1.25 and can be bought at the electronic kiosk before boarding.

Visas & Customs

EU residents do not need an entry visa. Residents of countries signed up to the Schengen Agreement (that's the EU minus the UK and Ireland but including Norway and Iceland) do not even need a passport to enter, and can swan through on a national ID card.

Tourist Information

Barcelona Airport Tourist Office	El Prat Airport	93 478 47 04
Barcelona Tourist Office (Cultural Events)	La Rambla	93 316 10 00
Plaça de Catalunya Tourist Information	Plaça d'Catalunya	93 285 38 34

Residents of Australia, Canada, Japan, New Zealand, Singapore, the United States and many South American countries may stay for holidays of up to 90 days without entry visas, but must present a valid passport. The length of passport validity needed varies. Residents of other countries must submit a visa application at the Spanish Embassy or consulate in their home country.

For more information and to download a form, go to the Ministro de Asuntos Exteriores y de Cooperación site (www.maec.es) and follow the links to your home country's consulate and visa section.

Visitor Information

There are five main tourist offices in the city. The biggest is under Plaça de Catalunya on the El Corte Inglés side of the square: look for the red signs. Multilingual staff are available from 09:00 to 21:00 every day. Others are at the Columbus monument, outside terminals A and B of Barcelona El Prat Airport, and Sants Station.

Embassies & Consulates

Australia	93 490 90 13
Austria	91 556 53 15
Belgium	93 467 70 80
Brazil	93 488 22 88
Canada	93 412 72 36
China	93 254 11 96
Denmark	93 488 02 22
Finland	93 443 15 98
France	93 317 81 50
Germany	93 292 10 00
Greece	93 321 28 28
Holland	93 363 54 20
Hungary	93 405 19 50
India	90 290 10 10
Ireland	93 491 50 21
Italy	93 467 73 05
Japan	93 280 34 33
Mexico	93 201 18 22
New Zealand	93 209 03 99
Norway	93 218 49 83
Poland	93 322 72 34
Portugal	93 318 81 50
Russian Federation	93 204 02 46
Sweden	93 488 25 01
Switzerland	93 409 06 50
United Kingdom	93 366 62 00
United States	93 280 22 27

Local Knowledge

Climate

Barcelona enjoys cool, clement winters, hot summers and year-round sun. January and February are the coolest months, averaging 10°C with occasional rain. August temperatures average 25°C, and occasionally hit the high 30s, which can feel unbearable.

October can be wet and stormy, but temperatures will generally remain mild. Fortunately, Barcelona has a growing army of umbrella salesmen, who seem to come out of the shadows as soon as you are caught in a shower.

Crime & Safety

Violent crime is rare, but bag-snatching and pick-pocketing are major concerns, particularly in the streets around La Rambla. The beaches, metro and rail network are other common spots for robberies, so keep your eyes open and your wits about you in all these places. Crime is generally petty, but muggings are not unknown in deserted streets late at night.

With a little vigilance, it's easy to avoid being a victim of crime. Never leave handbags or valuables lying around on tables or on the floor as, sooner or later, they will disappear. Keep your camera close to you, don't leave valuables in the outer pockets of your bag or coat and be extra careful when using ATMs.

The Mossos d'Esquadra police force is very visible around La Rambla, and can help in an emergency. The general emergency number is 112.

Dos & Don'ts

Each bar, restaurant and public space has its own policy on smoking, so check beforehand. Drinking alcohol on the street is prohibited, although it's still very common.

Queuing is more orderly than it seems. The custom is to ask who is last (*qui és l'últim?*), and wait until whoever answered has had their go. In bars and clubs, however, it is often every man for himself.

Spaniards tend to skip the perpetual apologising and excusing of some other European countries. 'Sorry' and 'thank you' are usually optional.

Men and women greet with a kiss on each cheek, even in formal situations. The same is true when two women meet. Meanwhile men just offer a handshake.

Dress codes are relaxed, although strappy tops and shorts are frowned upon when visiting churches. Things can get chilly on winter evenings, so carry scarves and jumpers. Summer can get hot, so wear light, airy materials. In banks, malls and restaurants, air conditioning can be turbo-charged, meaning it's a good idea to carry an extra layer.

Electricity

Plugs in Spain are the round, two-pin ones that are also used in France and Italy. Make sure you purchase a plug adaptor before you travel, as these can be quite hard to find. The standard current is 220V, so be aware that current transformers are necessary for American appliances.

Female Visitors

It is advisable to not walk alone late at night, and certainly not in the back streets of Ciutat Vella, where handbag theft is common. Getting public transport alone is not usually any cause for concern, although be vigilant when taking the *nitbus* (nightbus).

Catcalls and comments are absolutely normal for women walking alone in the street; they're intended as a compliment, and ignoring them will not cause offence. There may be some individuals who try to force conversation, but if you're feeling harrassed then attract the attention of other people. Wear whatever you're comfortable in, but bear in mind that fewer clothes usually equals more attention, and in Barcelona there's no shortage of male attention.

Language

Barcelona is a bilingual city, using both Catalan and Spanish almost equally. Street and shop signs are in Catalan and menus tend to be in both languages, although around La Rambla French, English and German translations are also common. The standard of English in city centre bars and restaurants is good, although it's always an idea to learn at least a few words and pleasantries, as this will be appreciated by the locals.

Lost Or Stolen Property

Missing valuables might just turn up in the city lost property office (Oficina de Troballes, Plaça Carles Pi i Sunyer, 8-10 or call 010). If you lose your passport you can apply for a temporary

Basic Spanish & Catalan

English	Spanish	Catalan
General		
Yes	Si	Si
No	No	No
Please	Por favor	Si us plau
Thank you	Gracias	Graciès
Good morning/hello	Buenos dias	Bon dia
Goodbye	Adios	Adeu
Questions		
How much?	Cuanto es?	Cuant és?
When?	Cuando?	Cuan?
Where is?	Donde esta?	On es?
What time is it?	Qué hora es?	Que hora és?
Getting Around		
Is this road to	Este es el camino a	És quest el camí a
Stop	Parada	Parar
Airport	Aeropuerto	Aeroport
Hotel	Hotel	Hotel
Restaurant	Restaurante	Restaurant
Numbers		
One	Uno(a)	Un(a)
Two	Dos	Dos (dues)
Three	Tres	Tres

Four	Cuatro	Cuatre
Five	Cinco	Cinc
Six	Seis	Sis
Seven	Siete	Set
Eight	Ocho	Vuit
Nine	Nueve	Nou
Ten	Diez	Deu
Eleven	Once	Onze
Twelve	Doce	Dotze
Thirteen	Trece	Tretze

Accidents

Police	Policia	Policia
Licence	Licencia	Llicencia
Accident	Accidente	Accident
Papers	Papeles	Papers
Insurance	Seguro	Assegurança
Sorry	Lo siento	Ho sento
Hospital	Hospital	Hospital
Doctor	Doctor	Metge
Ambulance	Ambulancia	Ambulància

one at your consulate or embassy (p.21). These should also help if you lose all your money and bank cards. For lost luggage at the airport, call 90 240 47 04, 24 hours a day. For emergencies, call the airport police on 93 297 12 19. For any items left in taxis, call 90 210 15 64. For belongings lost on the metro or buses, call 93 318 70 74.

Money

Spain uses the euro, and cash and major credit cards are the most common forms of payment. However, you'll need to show some form of photo ID, such as a driving licence or passport, when paying with plastic. Many smaller shops, bars, market stalls and restaurants will not take cards or high-value notes.

Banks and ATMs are plentiful, but banks close in the afternoons and at weekends. There are moneychangers on La Rambla that will accept travellers' cheques. Some banks also offer this service; check for the sign on the door. ATM networks are compatible with most international systems, such as Cirrus, American Express, Visa, MasterCard and Plus.

People With Disabilities

Barcelona's wheelchair access is patchy. The airport and most tourist attractions are accessible, although Park Güell can be tough to navigate. Many restaurants will have accessible toilets, but it is worth checking when you book.

Most buses now have adapted facilities: look for the wheelchair sign. The metro, sadly, is a different story: only Line 2 has lifts in all stations, although there are plans to improve. Street navigation is generally fine, with lots of ramps, and parking areas have spaces for drivers with disabilities.

Police

Barcelona has four police forces; the Guardia Urbana are the city police who wear sky blue and navy, while the Mossos d'Esquadra are the Catalan police and wear blue and red. The

Policía Nacional (blue combat clothes) and the Guardia Civil (green and black) are both state police forces. All are armed and any of them will help out in an emergency. The number to call is 112.

Post & Courier Services

Spain's postal service is called Correos and local post offices can be found on their website (www.correos.es). Stamps can be bought from most tobacconists, and from the yellow-bannered post offices. Postboxes are bright yellow. In theory, letters take around four working days to reach other European destinations and eight working days to get to the US and Australia. However, this is extremely variable.

Public Toilets

Public toilets are scarce in Barcelona, although all the beaches apart from one (Nova Icària) will have them. When caught short, it shouldn't be a problem to nip into a bar and use theirs, but this is down to the discretion of the manager.

Telephone & Internet

The cheapest way to make international calls is to use a *locutorio* (internet cafe) or international calling card. The latter can be bought in tobacconists and internet cafes. Internet access is good, and the scruffy *locutorios* normally have the best rates. Generally, €1.50 an hour is a good deal. Because of the density of the city, it's often possible to hop onto someone else's Wi-Fi signal.

Cyclists on the Rambla del Mar

Time

Spain is one hour ahead of GMT. Shops open at 10:00, often take a siesta between 14:00 and 17:00 and close at 21:00. Market stalls open from 07:00 to 14:00. Business hours are 09:00 to 19:00, with a two-hour lunch break from 14:00. Banks don't re-open after lunch. Restaurants open from 13:00 to 17:00 and then from 20:00 to late. Bars get busy at midnight, while clubs only pick up at 02:00. Most businesses close on Sundays. Museums and most restaurants close on Mondays, and many businesses shut for a chunk of August. There are 15 public holidays, which often catch visitors unawares (see p.34).

Tipping

Tips are appreciated, but not expected. For waiters, locals often leave loose change or round up to the nearest note. A euro or two is enough for taxi drivers and hotel staff.

Media & Further Reading

Newspapers & Magazines

Local and international magazines and newspapers are easy to find. In the city centre, many international titles are sold at newspaper kiosks. Expect to pay €2 to €3 during the week for foreign papers.

There are several local English language titles: *Catalonia Today* (www.cataloniatoday.cat) is a weekly newspaper (€2) highlighting key regional news and events. *Barcelona Metropolitan* (www.barcelona-metropolitan.com) is a free, A4 sized monthly magazine targeting expats and has features on local issues and detailed listings. Look for it in local bars, cafes and restaurants. *Barcelona Connect* (www.barcelonaconnect.com) is another freebie (A5), with detailed listings. Papers such as *The Guardian*, *New York Times* and *The Telegraph* are most likely to be found in tourist areas, but are becoming increasingly popular in residential areas.

Television

All terrestrial channels picked up in Barcelona are in Spanish or Catalan. Films and comedies originally in English can be viewed undubbed by hitting the 'original version' mode on your remote control.

Television Espanola (TVE) offers TVE 1, which is mainly entertainment and news, and TVE 2, which is more highbrow, with some drama and children's programming.

Most of the English and Irish bars in the city centre have large screens and will show major sporting events; these are often advertised in advance with signs outside the door.

Montjuïc Communications Tower

Media & Further Reading

Radio

There is no English-language radio station, and broadcasts tend to be in ferociously rapid Spanish or Catalan. Radio National de España offers Radio 1 (88.3FM), which is talk, news and music, Radio Classica (93FM), which offers classical music and Radio 3 (98.6FM), which is eclectic local rock and pop, and Flamenco, rap, folk and world music.

Books & Maps

You can deepen your appreciation of the city with *Barcelona and Modernity: Picasso, Gaudí, Miró, Dalí,* a hefty hardcover on the city's art and architecture, or lick your lips as you browse *Catalan Cooking* by Coleman Andrews. For history and politics, grab a copy of the classic *Homage to Catalonia,* George Orwell's personal account of the Spanish civil war, or Colm Tóibín's *Homage to Barcelona*, which ties together the city's rich history with its democratic transition after Franco. *Barcelona* is an opinionated stroll through the city's violent history by Aussie scribe Robert Hughes. Carlos Ruiz Zafón's thriller *Shadow of the Wind* hit the best-seller lists, and Ildefonso Falcones' *The Cathedral of the Sea*, soon to be translated into English, has proved popular among locals. Maps are available from most news-stands and tourist information centres.

Useful Websites & Blogs

Blogs are increasingly popular, especially in the football community, while there are a number of websites that are very useful for planning your trip.

Websites

City Information

www.bcn.cat	City hall services
www.bcn.cat/guia/welcome.htm	Excellent interactive city map
www.meteocat.com	Local weather
www.tmb.net	City transport network
www.turismedebarcelona.com	Tourism department

Entertainment & Culture

www.barceloca.com	Clubs, bars, museums
www.guiadelociobcn.es	'What's on' guide

News & Media

www.barcelonaconnect.com	Free monthly magazine
www.barcelona-metropolitan.com	Free monthly magazine
www.barcelonareporter.com	Catalan news in English
www.bcnweek.com	Free weekly magazine
www.lecool.com	Weekly listings email
www.typicallyspanish.com	National news in English

Directories

www.barcelona.angloinfo.com	Services listing in English
www.barcelonahotels.es	Hotels and reservations
www.barcelona-online.com	Services listing in English

Others

www.downloadalanguage.com	Useful Catalan and Spanish phrases
www.gencat.net	Catalan government
www.spainexpat.com	Expat information

Barcelona's reputation for partying is well-earned. With 15 public holidays and dozens of cultural festivals, there's always something going on.

Public Holidays

The locals love a good fiesta (or *festa* in Catalan) and the year is littered with excuses to spill into the street for drink, dance and a song. Republican, liberal Barcelona is less Catholic than other parts of Spain. The religious element of Christmas and Easter still remains important, and both are marked with parades, but are seen as times for the family rather than raucous revelry (though there's a bit of that too). The main Christmas celebration is the arrival of the Three Kings on January 6, rather than December 25. Just because Barcelona is agnostic, doesn't mean it will forego a day off: the Assumption, All Saints' Day and Day of the Immaculate Conception are all still holidays.

The big events tend to be celebrations of (Catalan) national pride. La Mercè (patron saint of Barcelona) is a three-day carnival of food, drink and music. The city also has a number of music festivals that are garnering international attention. Finally, too numerous to mention here, are the *festas* to be found in each *barri*. Often running within bigger events, each neighbourhood will celebrate at least once a year with fireworks, dancing, parades and plenty of music. Keep an eye on the local papers for details.

Public Holidays

January 1	New Year's Day
January 6	Epiphany
Good Friday	Changes annually
Easter Monday	Changes annually
May 1	Labour Day
Pentecost	Changes annually
August 15	Assumption
September 11	National Day of Catalonia
September 24	La Mercè
October 12	Columbus Day
November 1	All Saints' Day
December 6	Constitution Day
December 8	Day of the Immaculate Conception
December 25	Christmas Day
December 26	Saint Stephen's Day/Boxing Day

Annual Events

Barcelona International Jazz Festival   October
Various Locations   www.theproject.es
For almost four decades, the city's jazz festival has lured
high-profile international performers. It kicks off at the
end of October and runs for several weeks, with concerts
scattered around the city, in venues such as the Palau de la
Musica, L'Auditori and the Teatre Auditori Sant Cugat. Past
performers have included Paolo Conte and Sonny Rollins.

Carnaval

February – March

Various Locations   www.bcn.es/carnaval

Before the Christian calendar marks the Lenten period of fasting, there's Carnaval; the celebration of decadence and excess. Locals get decked out in costumes and join the parades marching through different neighbourhoods. The bigger, more flamboyant celebrations take place in the nearby beach town of Sitges.

Cavalcada dels Reis Mags d'Orient

January 5

Various Locations   www.barcelonaturisme.com

The Epiphany (the arrival of the Three Kings in the Nativity tale), is January 6, but the festivities kick off the night before. Kings Melchior, Caspar and Balthasar are greeted with huge fanfare, as the parade – often including live camels – winds its way through the city. Streets are packed with families, and kids scramble to collect sweets thrown from the elaborately-decorated floats.

Diada de Sant Jordi

April 23

Various Locations   www.bcn.es

This is the city's answer to Valentine's Day. Men give women a single long-stemmed rose, and women give men books. The day honours Catalonia's dragon-slaying patron saint, Sant Jordi (St George), with the red rose symbolising dragon blood. And the books? Miguel de Cervantes and William Shakespeare both died on this day in 1616. Book and rose stalls line the main streets, and the Catalan flag is displayed everywhere.

Performers on La Rambla

Festa de La Mercè

September

Various Locations

www.bcn.cat

Barcelona ends summer with the party of the year in honour of its patron saint, La Virgen de la Mercè. Expect hundreds of events, concerts, *castells* exhibitions, parades of fire-breathing dragons and devils, *sardana* dances and an air show. The official holiday is September 24, and the festival runs for several days before or after that date, usually corresponding with the closest weekend.

Festa Major de Gràcia

August

Various Locations

www.festamajordegracia.cat

Every neighbourhood has its own week of parties and events, and Gràcia hosts what is undisputedly the city's best. It's a week of free concerts in the squares, unofficial caipirinha bars on street corners, *correfocs* (costumed devils that run through the streets with sparklers) and a host of other activities, all taking place in fantastically decorated streets. Each year a coveted award goes to the best-decorated street.

Fira de la Santa Llúcia

December

Various Locations

www.bcn.cat

The Santa Llúcia market rings in the holidays at the start of December. Stalls lining the plaza are stocked with Nativity figures, mistletoe, Christmas trees and arts and crafts. These include some of the weirder Catalan traditions, such as the *caganer* (a little figurine who squats in Nativity scenes with his trousers round his ankles), and Caga Tió, a log with a face that is taken home by children in the run-up to Christmas and beaten until it 'poops' sweets and nuts.

Grec Festival
June – August
www.barcelonafestival.com

Various Locations
One of the city's most beloved festivals, the Grec's dance, music and theatre programme has been a summer highlight for more than three decades, with many concerts taking place outdoors. Performances are held throughout the city, and there are a number of kid-friendly events. It's usually held from mid-June through to the beginning of August, and the tourist office will have the updated schedule from around the end of May.

Primavera Sound
May – June
www.primaverasound.com

Parc del Forum, Sant Martí
One of the city's bigger music festivals, with more than 100 bands on the three-day line-up, Primavera Sound kicks off the summer season and has featured the likes of Lou Reed, Sonic Youth, the White Stripes and the Smashing Pumpkins. The past couple of events have been held at the Forum's seaside venue, but check out the website for upcoming dates and locations.

Santa Eulàlia
February
www.bcn.es/festa

Various Locations
Santa Eulàlia was one of the city's patron saints before being dethroned by Mercè in the 17th century, but she has not been forgotten. What the La Mercè feste does in summer,

Santa Eulàlia pulls off for the winter, although on a smaller and less raucous scale. The feast day is February 12 and the week is dedicated to the usual Catalan festival shenanigans, like *correfocs*, *castellers* and *gegants*. There is a craft fair and children's activities outside the cathedral, where Santa Eulàlia is buried.

Sónar
June

Various Locations
www.sonar.es

This three-day music and multimedia festival has become famous across Europe for its challenging, cutting-edge programme of electronic music, new media and audiovisual displays. Daytimes are taken up with eclectic and frequently odd acts in the MACBA courtyard, while the epic night-time sessions have achieved legendary status among dance music fans. Advance purchase is recommended. Visit www.ticktackticket.com.

Summercase
July

Fòrum, Poblenou
www.summercase.com

With the glistening Mediterranean as a backdrop, the long summer nights sizzle with Summercase's crowd-pleasing line-up of rock, pop and dance acts. Tag-teaming with similar concerts in Madrid, around 50 acts play Barcelona's Fòrum during the Friday and Saturday event. Although the event is still pretty new, it has rapidly established itself on the festival calendar with the likes of Daft Punk, Arcade Fire and the Chemical Brothers.

The combustable Festa Major de Gràcia (©iStockphoto.com/Georgia Davey)

Getting Around

While the bustling city centre is best explored on foot, there are plenty of ways to discover the rest of Barcelona.

Barcelona is an easy city to navigate. The streets of Eixample are set out in a grid, and many sights within the labyrinthine alleys of the Ciutat Vella are within walking distance of each other. There is an efficient and expansive public transport network, comprising buses, a metro, suburban rail network, glitzy tramlines, funicular railways and cable cars. There are also bus routes specifically for tourists. Metro and bus services are all frequent and fairly quick. Single fares on buses, trams and the metro are €1.25, but a T-10 ticket (€6.90) is better value, allowing 10 journeys that can combine all three modes of transport. Tickets can be shared between several passengers, but they must be validated when boarding trams or buses. See box, right, for prices.

For short trips and when exploring the Ciutat Vella, the best way to get about is on foot. The atmospheric streets mean that, even if your journey is meandering and the winding streets are confusing, it'll still be fun.

Bicycle

With its temperate climate and large areas of relatively flat terrain, Barcelona is well-suited to cycling. The city is building more cycle paths and drivers are gradually becoming more considerate, but Amsterdam this ain't, and any trip on two wheels requires that you keep your wits about you. The shiny red bikes of Bicing, the municipal bike-hire scheme, are off-limits to tourists, but there are plenty of bike tour places, including Fat Tire (93 301 3612, Carrer Escudellers 48, www.fattirebiketoursbarcelona.com) and Budget Bikes (93 304 18 85, Carrer del Marquès de Barberà 15, www.budgetbikes.eu). The Barcelona tourism office (93 285 38 32, www.barcelonaturisme.com) has a list of bike rental companies and recommended routes.

Bus

A frequent, reliable network covers the city, linking to other transport modes. Weekend and night services (*nitbus*) are slightly less reliable. Route maps and schedules are posted at most bus stops, and Transports Metropolitans de Barcelona (93 223 51 51, www.tmb.net) has an online journey planner. Tickets need to be validated on boarding. Drivers may change small notes onboard, but it's best to try and have the correct money just in case. TMB also runs three tourist routes, with hop-on, hop-off buses that take in 44 of the biggest attractions (€19 for one day, or €23 for two).

Travel Cards

Targetes allow travel on the metro, trains, buses and FGC. One 'trip' covers an hour and 15 minutes across all forms of transport. Prices below are for Zone 1.
T-Dia: €5.25 for one day
T-10: €6.90 for 10 trips
T-50: €28.60 for 50 trips
Tickets can be bought from electronic kiosks in stations, and you can pay with cash or credit card.

Boat

Boat travel takes a few different shapes, from cruise ships to the Balearic Islands, to tours of the city's shoreline and port. Operators docked near Moll d'Espanya and Port Vell (Map 11) will take you out on the sea for a few hours and explain Barcelona's coastal history. Las Golondrinas (www.lasgolondrinas.com) is here and does runs to nearby beaches. Turisme de Barcelona has listings of operators and the type of tours on offer (93 285 38 32, www.barcelonaturisme.com).

Metro

Barcelona's colour-coded and well-signed metro (93 318 70 74, www.tmb.net) provides a rapid, frequent and reliable service between the city's neighbourhoods, with good connections to bus and train lines. Single fares are €1.25; but the multi trip *targetes* are better value, especially the T-10, which can be used with other transport services. See the box on p.43 for more details.

Trains runs every three to five minutes, from 05:00 to midnight on Sundays to Thursdays, and from 05:00 until 02:00 the following morning on Fridays and Saturdays. The city has been testing 24 hour service on Saturdays, with the trial period ending in late 2007. As this book went to print, there was no decision on the continuation of this. The metro is relatively safe, but pickpocketing is common on the busier sections of the line; keep an eye on your possessions and don't store valuables in easy-to-reach places.

Clockwise from top left: Telefèric de Montjuïc, Tibidabo's trams, a Trixi Tour for two

Essentials

Teleféric de Montjuïc

Trixi Tour = 6 €

Rail

There are several rail firms. Both Cercanies Renfe (www.renfe.es/cercanies, 902 240 202) and FGC (Ferrocarrils de la Generalitat de Catalunya, www.fgc.es, 93 205 15 15) serve the outlying suburbs and run to satellite towns like El Prat, Gavà, Sitges, Terrassa and Mataró. For FCG information, visit the firm's website or the information desks in the stations at Plaça de Catalunya, Plaça d'Espanya and Provença. For Cercanies information, visit Passeig de Gràcia or Plaça de Catalunya stations, or get online. Bear in mind that Plaça de Catalunya's station has two sections, one for Cercanies and one for FCG; check the logo on the sign before descending.

Renfe is the national rail service, and runs trains (including sleepers) to

Scooting About

To truly feel like a local, you will need a scooter. These ubiquitous, buzzing runabouts may still be considered a little nerdy in the English-speaking world, but Barcelonins manage to make them look very hip. You're as likely to see suited business folk on one as modish media types or canoodling teenagers. This is primarily because they make getting around the city so easy, and can even navigate the tiny alleys of the Ciutat Vella. And they really do look very cool. The firms below specialse in scooters: BarcelonaMoto.com (600 370 343), Motissimo (93 490 84 01), Mopeds to Rent (97 234 13 10) or Vanguard (93 439 38 80).

France and the far reaches of Spain. See www.renfe.es for more information. The site is in English and Spanish.

Self-Drive

With its congestion, traffic jams, narrow Ciutat Vella streets and parking nightmares, Barcelona can be tricky for drivers. But the grid system gives some orientation, and main avenues pull traffic to the bigger highways. Cars drive on the right, and ferociously fast. An orange traffic light is generally assumed to mean 'hurry up', and people will start revving their engines long before they turn green. The speed limit varies between 30kph in some residential areas, up to 120kph on the motorways. It is widely ignored.

Hiring A Car

Many car hire companies have offices at the airport, by the port and by bus and train stations. Hotels will often assist with bookings as well. Base day rates vary widely, depending on the season, demand and car type.

Car Rental Agencies

Avis	93 298 36 00	www.avis.es
BCN Rent a Car	93 490 19 30	www.bcnrentacar.com
Blai Limousines	93 303 43 34	www.blailimousines.com
EasyCar	90 629 28 27	www.easycar.com
Europcar IB	93 491 48 22	www.europcar.com
The Golden Wheels	93 364 44 33	www.thegoldenwheels.com
Hertz	93 298 33 00	www.hertz.com

Taxi

Barcelona's regulated black and yellow taxis are reasonably affordable, and particularly useful after midnight, when public transport is limited. Drivers are usually friendly and honest, but their English can vary, so you may want to write down the address of

Taxi Companies	
Barcelona Taxi Van	670 531 619
Fonotaxi	93 300 11 00
Radio Taxi 033	93 303 30 33
Servitaxi	93 330 03 00

your destination. Vacant taxis have a green light and can be flagged down. Head to an intersection for the best chances of nabbing one. Alternatively, you can call one (see table above), but will have to pay a small supplement.

Taxis use meters. Fares start at €1.75, and then 78 cents per kilometre. This increases to €1.85, and €1 per kilometre at night, weekends, holidays and on airport trips.

Tram

Trams (www.trambcn.com, 90 219 32 75) are a recent addition to the city's transport network, with three lines running along parts of Diagonal and Parc de la Ciutadella.

Walking

Barcelona is a town for walkers. Pavements on even the narrowest streets are adequate, and many of the main boulevards are designed with leisurely strolls in mind. Much of the city is flat, but if you want an extra challenge, head

Glòries Metro, by Torre Agbar

for the hilly parks Güell, Montjuïc and Tibidabo. Most places are pedestrian-friendly, although at night you may want to take extra care. Local tourist offices (p.20) can provide suggestions for walking routes and maps.

Places To Stay

From medieval palaces and glitzy hotels to family-run hotels, there's plenty of choice for a place to rest your head.

Barcelona has accommodation to suit most tastes and budgets. The biggest concentration is around the Ciutat Vella, while many of the more upmarket hotels are along Passeig de Gràcia and in Eixample.

The star ranking system is widely used and prices are competitive, but can vary sharply depending on the location, season, and the timing of conferences or cultural events. For a double room at a four or five star hotel, prices start at around €200 and can rise to €2,500 per night. Moderate two and three star hotels and two star hostels, sometimes called *hostales* (not to be confused with youth hostels) cost between €50 and €200 per night. They tend to be comfortable and clean, with en-suite bathrooms, although the atmosphere and decor can vary greatly. Youth hostel dorm beds cost €20 to €25. It's worth asking about seasonal discounts. Visit the Barcelona Hotel Association (www.barcelonahotels.es) and Turisme de Barcelona (www.barcelonaturisme.com) for more information.

Price Guide
€ – Less than €100
€€ – €101 to €200
€€€ – €201+
The euro sign is intended to give a rough idea on costs. These are based on prices in mid 2007 for a double room, and are subject to change.

Abba Sants Hotel

www.abbasantshotel.com

93 600 31 00

Don't let the exterior's functional look fool you. Inside you'll find comfortable business class accommodation with Wi-Fi, massage services and satellite TV. Good for short stopovers in the city.

AC Miramar

www.slh.com

93 281 16 00

This newcomer on the high-end hotel scene only opened in October 2006. Its Montjuïc location is a hike to get to, but the stunning sea, city and garden views make it a notable urban retreat.

€€

Barceló Hotel Atenea Mar

www.bchoteles.com

93 531 60 40

This is in the redevelopment zone by Fòrum Barcelona, but it's an area that is establishing an identity. The La Nova Mar Bella beach and the Diagonal Mar shopping centre are within easy reach.

€

Ciutat Barcelona Hotel

www.ciutathotels.com

93 269 74 75

Little details such as bathrobes, and a fresh (although basic) decor give this mid-range hotel the feel of a much more expensive establishment. The central location and free bottled water push up the charm factor.

 €

Gran Hotel La Florida

www.hotellaflorida.com

93 259 30 00

Far from the noise, on a hill overlooking the city, this is where James Stewart and Ernest Hemingway chose to stay. Closed in 1979, it reopened in 2003 after a major renovation, and remains one of the city's plushest hotels.

 €€€

Hostal Gat Xino

www.gataccommodation.

93 324 88 33

If you want a taste of Barcelona at its most gritty and eclectic, head here. This Raval classic is small and basic, but the design gives it a funky, fresh look. Great location for galleries, restaurants and bars.

 €

Hotel 1898

www.nnhotels.com

93 552 95 52

This 19th century building was once the headquarters of the Compañía de Tabacos de Filipinas. Now an upmarket hotel, it has lots of colonial touches and an elegant use of brick and wood creates a nostalgic feel.
€€

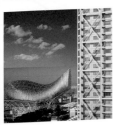

Hotel Arts Barcelona

www.ritzcarlton.com

93 221 10 00

The Arts is full-on luxury, with sensational service and facilities. With terraced gardens, Spanish art, a deluxe spa, outdoor pools and gourmet restaurants it's a spot for relaxation and indulgence.
€€€

Hotel Claris

www.derbyhotels.com

93 487 62 62

Housed in the renovated 19th century Verduna Palace, the hotel is one block from Passeig de Gràcia. It has 124 stylishly decorated rooms. Extras include a rooftop pool and a collection of Egyptian artefacts.
€€

Hotel Colón

www.hotelcolon.es

93 301 14 04

You can't get much closer to the cathedral than this. Many of the rooms have views of the Gothic church, and Mercat de Santa Caterina is a few streets away. Rooms are bright and cheery.

€€

Hotel Majestic

www.hotelmajestic.es

93 488 17 17

As the name implies, the Majestic exudes old-school charm. The facade, dating back to 1918, blends in with its Gaudí-influenced neighbours. It has a Michelin-starred restaurant and a terrace with a pool.

€€

Prestige Paseo de Gracia

www.prestigepaseodegracia.com

93 272 41 80

Its minimalist design makes this boutique hotel stand out from other trendy, city-centre hideaways. Spacious interior patios, Bang & Olufsen TVs and good use of natural lighting add to the sophistication.

€€

Hotels

Three & Four Star

Hotel del Mar	93 319 33 02	www.gargallo-hotels.com
Hotel Jazz	93 552 96 96	www.nnhotels.com
Hotel Nouvel	93 301 82 74	www.hotelnouvel.com
Torre Catalunya	93 600 69 99	www.expogrupo.com

Two Star

Hostal d'Uxelles	93 265 25 60	www.hotelduxelles.com

Hotel Apartments & Guesthouses

Hotel Apartments

Barcelona has hundreds of apartments available on short lets. Fully furnished and self-catering facilities are sometimes ranked by suns instead of stars. Amenities, such as parking, 24 hour security, and cleaning services vary widely.

Stays can be daily (usually with a two or three-day minimum), weekly, monthly or longer. For shorter stays, prices are comparable to hotels, but discounts are typically available on long-term contracts.

To get started, the Associació d'Apartaments Turístics de Barcelona (www.apartur.com) and Turisme de Barcelona (www.barcelonaturisme.com) list companies, and the Barcelona Hotels Association (www.barcelonahotels.es) has an online reservation system.

Hotel Apartments

Desigbarcelona	93 467 67 74	www.desigbarcelona.com
Lofts & Apartments	93 268 33 88	www.lofts-apartments.com
MH Apartments Managers SL	93 323 87 90	www.mhapartments.com
Qualitur Consulting	93 485 04 24	www.feelathomeinbarcelona.com
Urban Flats	93 215 01 96	www.urban-flats.com

Guesthouses

Phrases like 'guesthouse', 'bed & breakfast', 'inn' and 'pension' are sometimes interchanged, and the traditional distinctions are greyer here than in other places. Even apartments and boats call themselves B&Bs. While they tend to have fewer amenities than their hotel counterparts, these places are cosier, more personal and may be part of a flat or take up an entire floor in a building. Some, but not all, offer en-suite facilities. Prices and quality vary. See BnB Finder (www. bnbfinder.com) for more information.

Guesthouses & Hostels

Ana's Guest House	93 459 18 43	www.anasguesthouse.com
Nisia Bed & Breakfast	93 415 39 60	www.nisiabcn.com
Willowmoon	93 484 23 65	www.willowmoon.uk.com

Hostels

Ideal Youth Hostel	93 342 61 77	www.idealhostel.com
Pere Tarrés	93 410 23 09	www.peretarres.org/alberg
Sea Point Youth Hostel	93 231 20 45	www.seapointhostel.com

Inside Casa Batlló

Exploring

Lost In Catalonia

Gleaming business districts, fairytale architecture, ancient streets, grand avenues, Barcelona has it all – and then there are the beaches.

Barcelonins like to say that, since the city has the sea on one side and the mountains on the other, it's impossible to get lost. This is not strictly true. Although much of the city has wide, grid-like streets where it's hard to lose your bearings, the Ciutat Vella (literally 'old city') is a dense, shady maze of sidestreets, alleys and cul-de-sacs, and tricky for newcomers to navigate.

Ciutat Vella is a blanket term that covers the areas once contained within the city walls: trendy, well-preserved Born, slightly tattier Sant Pere (grouped together on p.70), the ancient Barri Gòtic (p.64) and lively Raval (p.74). The Barri Gòtic and Raval are divided from one another by La Rambla (p.64). These three areas have many of the city's bars and restaurants (see Going Out, p.154).

A spit hanging from the bottom of Born forms the old fisherman's district of Barceloneta (p.78), which is flanked by the beach and marinas, including Port Olímpic.

The city didn't expand beyond its walls until the 19th century, when the distinctive grid that makes up much of the rest of the city, the Eixample ('extension'), was built. The Eixample (p.90) runs from Ciutat Vella towards the hill; it's a solidly bourgeois residential district with many Moderniste buildings, including Gaudí's Sagrada Familia (p.93). It's home to museums and galleries, and one of the city's most emblematic shopping streets, Passeig de Gràcia (see p.138).

Avinguda Diagonal, a major road that bisects the city, separates Eixample from the districts further up the hill (Above Eixample, p.202). These were separate towns until Eixample swallowed them, and include wealthy (and slightly snooty) Sarrià-Sant Gervasi, and trendy Gràcia, which has a more bohemian feel. The area is home to many attractions, including Park Güell (p.98) and the CosmoCaixa science museum (p.96). There are also a number of bars and restaurants that are well worth the trip (see Going Out, p.154).

The rugged hill that rises from the shoreline towards the airport is Montjuïc, one of Barcelona's few green spaces. It's home to many galleries, including the Fundació Miró (p.85) and is the site of the Olympic facilities (p.86).

We've picked the best of the city, organised into areas, to make exploring easy. But, perhaps the best way to get a feel for Barcelona is to wander the streets and discover your own hidden gems. For eating and drinking options, see Going Out (p.154).

Ticket To Ride

Barcelona's public transport system is extensive, and inexpensive. Taxis are cheap and plentiful, but you will rarely need one near the centre of town. The first thing visitors should do is buy a *targeta*. These tickets allow multiple journeys by bus, tram, metro and train. See p.42 for more.

At A Glance

On the following pages, the city has been carved into different areas to make it more manageable. Here, sights are listed by type.

Heritage Sights

Museums & Art Galleries

Beaches & Parks

Sights & Attractions

Barri Gòtic

The city's ancient core has been built and rebuilt over two millennia, making it a fascinating tapestry of Barcelona's past.

Bustling and charming, the Barri Gòtic lies on top of an original Roman settlement, and remains the city's administrative and commercial heart. Bordered by the iconic, kilometre-long boulevard La Rambla (below) on one side and Via Laietana on the other, it stretches from Plaça de Catalunya to the sea in a dense mesh of breathtaking medieval streets and tiny plaças, with the expansive Plaça Sant Jaume somewhere near the centre. The best way to explore the district is by setting off on long, ambling walks in the ancient backstreets, soaking up the unique atmosphere.

For **restaurants and bars** in the area, see p.164.

For **shopping**, see El Corte Inglés, p.142 Barri Gòtic, p.136 and Portal de l'Àngel, p.136.

La Rambla

Plaça de Catalunya to the sea

www.bcn.net

The strip leading from Plaça de Catalunya to the Columbus monument is an exhilarating blast of human activity, with plenty to distract you from the beautiful buildings. A leisurely ramble down La Rambla takes you past the Canaletes fountain (where Barça supporters gather after major victories), through a cacophony of live bird, animal and flower stalls, past the entry to the Boqueria market (p.140), along an avenue of human statues and artists selling their

Inside La Seu Cathedral

works. The last stretch before the sea often hosts buskers and breakdancers. Put simply, it's unmissable. 🔲 Catalunya, Map 7

La Seu Catedral
Pl de la Seu

93 315 15 54
www.website.es/catedralbcn

Barcelona's cathedral is one of the great Gothic buildings of Iberia. Work began in 1298 and was completed in 1448, although a final flourish was added to the front in the 1880s. The interior, which has 29 chapels, is impressive, but the best feature is the cloister courtyard, complete with palm trees and a gaggle of geese. A €5 donation is requested for admission. 🔲 Jaume I, Map 10 A1 🔳

Museu d'Història de la Ciutat
Pl del Rei

93 315 11 11
www.museuhistoria.bcn.es

The lift to the excavation site below the museum counts down the years as you descend, finishing at -12, the BC era when Barcino was founded by the Romans. The city remains are impressive and there is something quite magical about their underground setting. There are also interactive screens to show how the city once looked. The highlight of the above ground section is the historic Saló del Tinell hall. Entrance to the museum costs €5. 🔲 Jaume I, Map 10 A2 🔳

Museu Frederic Marès
Pl de la Seu, 5-6

93 310 58 00
www.museumares.bcn.cat

Frederic Marès was a sculptor, historian and teacher, but most of all he was an obsessive collector. Kids might dismiss the medieval sculptures and crucifixes on the ground floor, but they'll adore the top floor, with its displays of old toys and games, playing cards, miniature theatres, fans, clocks, keys and pipes. The museum costs €3 to enter, and is housed in the former Royal Palace of the Counts.

Urquinaona, Map 10 A1 **3**

Palau de la Virreina

La Rambla, 99

93 316 10 00
www.barcelona.es

This is an expansive 19th century townhouse built around a pretty courtyard. It has two art spaces: the Espai 2 usually shows contemporary art while the Espai Xavier Miserachs is generally dedicated to photography. A third gallery, called La Capella, is housed in the Antic Hospital de la Santa Creu at the back and focuses on new work by contemporary artists. Exhibitions tend to be compact and original and worth the €3 entrance fee. Catalunya, Map 7 D4 **4**

If you only do one thing in...
Barri Gòtic

Take a tour of the Grand Liceu theatre, which has been spectacularly rebuilt after it was destroyed in a fire (93 485 99 00, La Rambla 51, www.liceubarcelona.com, p.211).

Best for...

Eating: Head to Can Culleretes (p.167) for hearty Catalan food in an atmospheric restaurant where they've been serving customers since 1786.

Drinking: The lights are low and the cocktails are strong at the cosy lounge bar Ginger (p.170).

Shopping: If chain stores are your thing, head to Portal de l'Àngel (p.136) for the cut-price wonders of the Spanish high street.

Sightseeing: Duck into the alleyways by the cathedral and hope you're lucky enough to find Plaça de Sant Felip Neri (Map 9 F1).

Culture: Just a little off the beaten track lie some lovely and historic but undervisited churches: look out for the Romanesque church of Santa Anna (Map 7 F2).

Born & Sant Pere

Historic buildings and a very modern spirit characterise the reinvigorated Born, while scruffier Sant Pere has stayed truer to its roots.

This Ciutat Vella district, between the Barri Gòtic and the Parc de la Ciutadella, is full of contrasts. Born is the epitome of Barcelona's reinvention: its ancient streets hold some of the city's oldest buildings, but it's also a buzzing playground of hip shops, bars and restaurants. Sant Pere is slightly more down-at-heel, but it's home to two particularly stunning buildings, the Moderniste Palau de la Música Catalana (p.71) and the modern Mercat de Santa Caterina (p.141). It also gives a flavour of what the rest of Ciutat Vella was like a decade ago.

For restaurants and bars in the area, see p.170.
For shopping, see Carrer Rec, p.138 and Mercat de Santa Caterina, p.141 .

Barcelona Zoo

Parc de la Ciutadella

93 225 67 80
www.zoobarcelona.com

There are more than 7,000 animals from 500 different species at Barcelona Zoo, which makes for a fulfilling visit, but also means that some of the enclosures are a tight fit. Dolphins, monkeys, elephants, hippos and panthers are all present and correct, and there have recently been negotiations to obtain some pandas. For smaller children, there is a petting farm and there are plenty of areas to stop for refreshments. Adult price is €14.50, children €8.75. 🚇 Bogatell, Map 13 A4 5

Basílica de Santa Maria del Mar

93 310 23 90

Pl Santa Maria

www.bcn.es/turisme

The 12th century Santa Maria del Mar has been the focal point of Born for centuries. Its elegant proportions and bare interior make it a superbly peaceful space, and there is some wonderful stained glass. At the church front, a pretty square, known as the Fossar de les Moreres, marks the spot where the last defenders of the city were executed at the end of the War of the Spanish Succession, in 1714. 🚇 Jaume I, Map 10 C4 🄺

Museu Picasso

93 319 63 10

C/ de Montcada, 15-23

www.museupicasso.bcn.es

This museum has one of the world's most complete Picasso collections, with particularly strong examples of early works and Blue Period pieces. There are also frequent temporary exhibitions. The museum itself is in a gorgeous series of adjoining medieval merchants' mansions. Entrance to the permanent collection is €6 (an €8.50 ticket also gets you into the temporary show). Be prepared to queue in summer months. 🚇 Jaume I, Map 10 C2 🄼

Palau de la Música Catalana

90 244 28 82

C/ de St Pere Més Alt, 1

www.palaumusica.org

An utterly fabulous orgy of colour and embellishments. Columns are tiled with exotic flowers, every wood or stone surface is elaborately carved, and the busts of musical greats glare down. Small wonder that Lluís Domènech i Montaner's crowning glory is a UNESCO World Heritage Site. There are daily guided tours costing €9. 🚇 Urquinaona, Map 8 B3 🄸

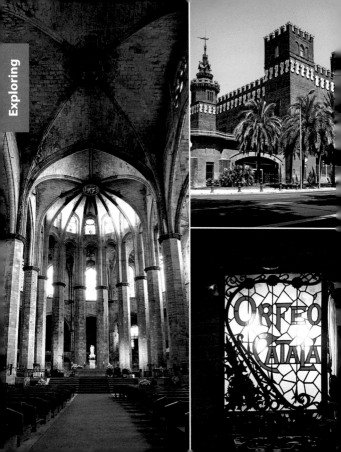

If you only do one thing in...
Born & Sant Pere

Stroll under the brickwork Arc de Triomf (Map 8 F3), which stands at the head of Passeig de Luís Companys, constructed for the 1888 World Exhibition.

Best for...

Eating: Taller de Tapas (p.175) offers excellent and authentic Spanish nibbles.

Drinking: If you're after cocktails then head to Gimlet (p.177) – but be prepared for a crush. Despite the bar's best efforts to keep a low profile, word has spread.

Sightseeing: It has to be the Picasso museum (p.71), for its bredth of work and impressive setting.

Culture: Take any chance you get to see a concert at Palau de la Música (p.71), if only to marvel at the interiors, with a pleasant classical-music soundtrack.

Families: Dragons and a mammoth are among the improbable beasts hiding in Parc de la Ciutadella (p.70).

Clockwise from left: Santa Maria del Mar church, the zooological museum, Palau de la Música Catalana

Raval

Once a no-go zone, Raval's come a long way in recent years, but remains an edgy, gritty *barri*.

The area to the left of La Rambla as you look up from the sea is one of the city's most colourful. Traditionally impoverished and crime-ridden, it was once home to the city's most accommodating bordellos and seediest bars. These days, it's home to huge immigrant communities and hip arty types, making it a vibrant, multicultural, anything-goes kind of place. The prettification of Raval has made it much safer, but there's still a seedy underbelly, especially on Carrer Sant Pau. Keep your wits about you and there's a treasure trove of attractions and some damn cool places to be discovered.

*For **restaurants and bars** in the area, see p.186.*
*For **shopping**, see MACBA area, p.137 and La Boqueria, p.140*

CCCB

C/ Montalegre, 5

93 306 41 00
www.cccb.org

Directly behind MACBA (p.75), the CCCB (Centre of Contemporary Culture for Barcelona) is housed in a former almshouse. The CCCB is a multi-discipline centre that holds temporary exhibitions, music shows, and film festivals. Exhibitions vary from the established to the experimental, of which many are mixed media. Exhibition entry costs €4.40. Out back is a café with loungers, while in the basement a bar opens up for events in the main hall. 🚇 Sant Antoni, Map 3 C2 9

MACBA

Pl dels Angels, 1

93 412 08 10
www.macba.es

Since opening in 1995, MACBA has been criticised as a victory of style over substance: it's suggested that the striking white building, designed by Richard Meier, is far more impressive than the exhibits inside. This is slightly unfair, although its dedication to experimentation occasionally leads to scrappy shows. Admittance to the permanent collection and any temporary shows is €7.50. 🚇 Catalunya, Map 7 C2 🔟

Museu Marítim

Av de les Drassanes

93 342 99 20
www.museumaritimbarcelona.org

This museum pays heritage to Barcelona's rich seafaring heritage, with a huge array of model ships, nautical instruments, a fine selection of ancient maps and, most impressively, a full-size replica of a royal galley on show. The museum is housed inside the city's incredibly well-preserved medieval shipyards, the Reials Drassanes, which were used for shipbuilding until the mid-18th century and then used as an arsenal and artillery park. Entrance is €6.50. 🚇 Drassanes, Map 11 B1 🔢

Rambla de Raval

Rla de Raval

www.bcn.es

When the cramped housing was torn down in 1997, many were convinced that they were losing their homes to make room for high-class hotels. So far Rambla de Raval has remained relatively Raval-ish, with kebab shops, curry houses and cosy bars. There's change afoot though, and many are concerned that there's serious gentrification ahead. 🚇 Liceu, Map 9 A2

If you only do one thing in...
Raval

The Antic Hospital de la Santa Creu (Carrer Carme 47, Map 7 C4) is one of Raval's quietest corners. It was built as a hospital, on a site where the ill had been treated since at least the 11th century.

Best for...

Eating: Carmelita's (p.188) offers Catalan classics in a slickly-renovated old building.

Drinking: Head to Carrer Joaquím Costa (Map 7 B3) for a night's bar-hopping: there's something for every taste.

Shopping: The streets between La Rambla and the MACBA/CCCB complex are the city's top destination for street and alternative clothing. If you need a floor-length leather coat or a skull-encrusted wristband, this is where to come.

Culture: Raval has a thriving underground arts scene, where independent galleries rule. Try Miscelänea (93 317 9398, C/ Guàrdia 10) or Galeria dels Àngels (93 412 54 54, C/ dels Àngels 16) for exhibitions by local artists.

Clockwise from top left: the maritime museum, a Raval alleyway and MACBA

Barceloneta & The Beaches

Beaches and marinas flank this atmospheric former fisherman's district, while the *barri* itself is home to a tight-knit, traditional community.

Barceloneta and the seafront are two of the city's most popular areas, but it hasn't always been so. Before preparations for the Olympics got underway, the seafront was a filthy, neglected wasteland bordered by the railway and ring road. Barceloneta, meanwhile, was a straggly, working-class suburb. The train tracks and motorway were buried however, and kilometres of beach were created, as were broad promenades and marinas lined with restaurants and bars, and the Maremagnum shopping centre. Barceloneta itself has remained deeply traditional but now feels quaint and cherished, while the beaches have become a quintessential part of the Barcelona experience.

*For **restaurants and bars** in the area, see p.180.*
*For **shopping**, see Maremagnum, p.147*

Aquarium

93 221 74 74
www.aquariumbcn.com

Moll d'Espanya del Port Vell

The aquarium is on the commercial island in Port Vell, and is among the largest in Europe. The highlight is the Oceanari, an 80 metre long glass tunnel, which allows you to walk through a tank surrounded by sharks and hundreds of other fish. Other tanks illustrate other habitats,

showing everything from sea horses to penguins. There
are interactive zones catering both to younger and older
children. Admission costs €13 for adults and €9 for children
under 12.

🚇 Drassanes/Barceloneta, Map 11 F4 **16**

Barceloneta Beach

93 481 00 53
C/ de l'Almirall Cervera   www.bcn.cat/platges

The closest beach to the city centre, Barceloneta lies at the
end of Passeig Joan de Borbó. It's a busy, buzzing place,
with hordes of sun-worshippers, *xiringuito* bars providing
music and mojitos, and old men playing dominoes in the
shade, apparently unperturbed by the commotion around
them. There are information points and toilets (be prepared
to queue). Towards the Port Olímpic end, beneath the two
towers, lies a row of restaurants.

🚇 Barceloneta, Map 1 C4

IMAX Port Vell

93 225 11 11
Moll d'Espanya, 1   www.imaxportvell.com

Using impressive 3D technology to make images leap out of
the screen, IMAX is a reliable crowd-pleaser. The films shown
on Port Vell's three screens are often dubbed into Spanish
and Catalan, but don't let that put you off: they tend to be
double bills of spectacular, adrenaline-filled documentaries
on sharks or mountain peaks, where the commentary is far
less gripping than the footage and megawatt sound system.
Adult entry is €11.

🚇 Drassanes/Barceloneta, Map 12 A3 **17**

Museu d'Història de Catalunya

Pl de Pau Vila, 3

93 225 47 00
www.mhcat.net

This museum charts the region's history from pre-historic settlers, to the War of Succession and Catalonia's loss of independence in 1714, through to the Franco years and the 1979 Statute of Self-Government. The display is varied, from historic artifacts to everyday items, and there are interactive options. The building itself was once a harbour warehouse. Entry is €3. 🚇 Barceloneta, Map 12 C2 🔟

Sant Sebastià Beach

Off Pg de la Escullera

93 481 00 53
www.bcn.cat/platges

Tucked away at the end of the spit, Sant Sebastià is just far enough from the Guàrdia Urbana to make it an anything-goes area. It is not officially a nudist beach, but people get naked anyway. Others come here to smoke weed or just to enjoy the sense of freedom. There is a very mixed crowd, with a considerable gay contingent. 🚇 Barceloneta, Map 1 C4

Transbordador Aeri Cable Car

Torre de Sant Sebastia

93 225 27 18
www.bcn.cat

This 1.3km cable car route, completed in 1931, links the harbour with Montjuïc and offers stunning views of the city and the coast. There are three stops: the Sant Sebastià tower (at the beach of the same name), Jaume I Tower (outside the World Trade Centre), and the Miramar (on top of Montjuïc mountain). At its highest point, the car climbs 70m above street level. A round trip costs €12.50 per person.

🚇 Barceloneta, Map 1 C4

Nova Icària & Other Beaches

Various Locations

www.bcn.cat/platjas

Nova Icària, just after the Port Olímpic development, attracts a young, local crowd. It gets busy at peak times and is a prime people-watching spot, but as it is wide and curved, there's space for beach volleyball, frisbees and other horseplay. Walking away from the towers takes you to Bogatell beach, which is less busy and attracts more families (Metro Poblenou); on the other side of Bogatell is broad, chilled-out Marbella (Metro Poblenou), which has a nudist beach at one end.

If you only do one thing in...

Barceloneta & The Beaches

At the centre of the roundabout where La Rambla meets the sea, stands the Columbus Monument, where the explorer points out to sea from atop his column.

Best for...

Eating: For people-watching, as well as for one of the city's best paellas, Kaiku (p.182) is a winner.

Drinking: On balmy summer nights, the terrace at Fritz Mar (p.183) is lively but relaxed.

Shopping: The large shopping centre of Maremagnum (p.147) offers a decent selection of high-street brands.

Outdoor: The beaches are the star of the show: take your pick from crammed but fun Barceloneta (p.180), nudist Marbella (p.81) or easy-going Nova Icària (p.81).

Family: The technicolour tropical fish displays and penguin tank at the Aquarium (p.81) are great for kids.

Clockwise from top left: climbing frame near Maremagnum, Rambla del Mar, Port Vell

Barceloneta & The Beaches

Montjuïc & Poble Sec

The tranquil, grassy slopes of Montjuïc are home to many of the city's finest cultural attractions.

Montjuïc, the hill that looms over the industrial port, is mostly given over to recreation. Approached from Plaça d'Espanya, a grand thoroughfare punctuated with fountains leads up to MNAC (p.86), while paths lead off to other attractions and galleries. Montjuïc is also home to the former Olympic facilities (p.86). Sandwiched between Montjuïc and Raval, and spidering up the hillside, are the higgledy-piggledy streets of Poble Sec, a multicultural *barri* that's often overlooked, but has some good bars as well as some Indian and South American restaurants.

For **restaurants and bars** in the area, see p.190.

CaixaForum
Av Marquès de Comillas, 6-8

93 476 86 00
www.fundacio.lacaixa.es

The four art spaces of this gallery are located in a magnificent brick building that looks like a giant children's fort but is actually a lovingly refurbished textile factory. Exhibitions tend to be refreshing and interesting, with a particular emphasis on modern art and photography. In order to get between galleries you have to walk through the courtyards, which is fantastic as it emphasises the sense of adventure and exploration involved in visiting the gallery. Admission is free.

Espanya, Map 6 A1 19

Font Màgica de Montjuïc

Av Reina Maria Cristina s/n   www.bcn.es/fonts

This grand avenue leads to Montjuïc from Plaça d'Espanya, delivering one of Barcelona's iconic images; the 'magic fountains'. As classical themes blast from speakers, the fountains are bathed in coloured lights, with whirling jets of water 'dancing' to the music. It's cheesy, but undeniably pretty, and the displays draw delighted crowds. In the summer (May to September), they are 20:00 to midnight, Thursday to Sunday. The rest of they year they're 19:00 to midnight, Friday and Saturday only. 🚇 Espanya, Map 6 B1 20

Fundació Joan Miró

Av de Miramar, s/n   93 443 94 70

www.bcn.fjmiro.es

Up at the top of Montjuïc, this offers the best collection of work by Joan Miró found anywhere in the world. A selection of paintings, sculptures, tapestries, prints and sketches show the maestro's development as an artist, his favourite themes and preoccupations. The building itself is a treasure: a sleek 70s work by Josep Lluís Sert, with fantastic views from the surrounding gardens and refreshments in the courtyard cafe. Admission to the museum is €7.50.

🚇 Espanya, Map 6 A4 21

Jardí Botànic

C/ Doctor Font i Quer, 2   93 426 49 35

www.jardibotanic.bcn.es

The new Botanical Gardens are tucked away behind the Olympic Stadium, and are dedicated to the conservation and study of Mediterranean flora, although Australian, northern and southern African, Chilean, Californian and Canary Island plant-life all get a look in. The garden's design is uncompromisingly modern and a far cry from a traditional botanical garden, but is still restful, and does a good job of showcasing the compact collection. Admission is €3, except at weekends, when it's free. 🚇 Hostafrancs, Map 1 B4

MNAC
Palau Nacional

93 622 03 60
www.mnac.es

The Catalan National Art Museum is somewhere you could spend days inside and still not see everything. The extensive collection spans works by Catalan and Catalonia-connected artists from the 10th to 20th centuries. The range of medieval and Romanesque art is vast, with an outstanding collection of frescos, while there's also a notable collection of *modernisme* art. The building itself is also worthy of mention, with magnificent high ceilings and domed hallways. Entry is €8.50.
🚇 Espanya, Map 6 A3 22

Olympic Stadium
Passeig Olímpic

93 406 20 89
www.bcn.es

The Olympic Stadium's facade was originally constructed for the 1929 World Exhibition, although the inside was completely rebuilt for the Olympics. In the same complex is the Palau Sant Jordi, where many of the indoor events were held, the Picornell swimming pools, and Calatrava's elegantly curving tower. The stadium is currently being used as RCD Espanyol's temporary home ground. Tours of the Olympic facilities are available. 🚇 Espanya, Map 6 A3 23

Parc de Montjuïc

Montjuïc

93 413 24 00
www.bcn.es/parcsijardins

Parc de Montjuïc is 250 hectares of green space covering the Montjuïc mountain, and surrounding sporting and cultural spots. There are several gardens to explore. These include Jardins del Teatre Grec (inspired by the Hanging Gardens of Babylon), the Jardins de Joan Maragall and Montjuïc Park itself. Meanwhile, children will love the space that the Funicular passes over. ⬛ Espanya, Map 1 B4

Poble Espanyol

Marquès de Comillas

93 508 63 00
www.poble-espanyol.com

This model village was designed for the 1929 World Expo, to celebrate and promote Spain's many different architectural styles. There's a town hall, a church, a monastery and several houses around a central plaza, each in the building style of a different Spanish region. There are art exhibitions, street performers, theatre shows and games for children. Admission is €7.50 for adults and €4 for children over 7 years old.

⬛ Espanya, Map 6 A1 24

Refugi 307

C/ Nou de la Rambla, 169

93 256 21 00
www.museuhistoria.bcn.cat

During the Spanish Civil War, bombs from German and Italian planes rained on Barcelona, and residents built makeshift air-raid shelters. After the war, Franco ordered them to be destroyed, but some survived, and the shelter in Poble Sec is among the best preserved. An informative guided tour of the tunnels lasts about one hour and costs €3. ⬛ Paral·lel, Map 1 B4

If you only do one thing in...
Montjuïc & Poble Sec

The pioneering pavilion designed by Mies Van Der Rohe was meticulously reconstructed in the 80s and remains a design classic (Avinguda Marques de Comillas, Map 6 A1).

Best for...

Eating: For delicious Mediterranean food with knockout views look no further than Montjuïc El Xalet (p.194).

Drinking: Salsita's (p.194) is a bright and buzzing cocktail lounge, packed with a young, friendly crowd.

Families: Poble Espanyol (p.87) provides a flavour of the rest of Spain. It has a slightly theme-park feel, and is particularly good for families.

Culture: The huge but highly specialised collections of the MNAC (p.86) include a unique, painstakingly preserved set of Roman frescos.

Sightseeing: The Olympic facilities (p.86) on the far side of Montjuïc highlight Barcelona's position on the world stage.

From top: the magic fountain in full flow, the Olympic Stadium

Eixample

Ciutat Vella is only half of Barcelona's story. Eixample's grid-like streets are home to some of the city's most fanciful buildings.

Work started on Eixample, the uniform grid that was planned to relieve the cramped conditions of the ancient city, as the city was at the peak of its 19th century wealth. Many of its earliest buildings were flamboyant *modernisme* homes for the nouveau riche: over 150 such buildings lie in the Quadrat d'Or ('golden quarter') around the junction of Carrer Roger de Llúria and Carrer Consell de Cent (Map 4 E3). A little further away from the Ciutat Vella lie Gaudí's magnificent Sagrada Familia (p.93) and the Hospital de la Santa Creu i Sant Pau (p.92), another major *modernisme* building.

*For **restaurants and bars** in the area, see p.196.*
*For **shopping**, see Passeig de Gràcia, p.138.*

Casa Batlló

Pg de Gràcia, 43

93 488 06 66
www.casabatllo.es

In 1906, industrialist Josep Batlló hired Gaudí to spritz up an apartment block. The building's front shimmers in an undulating layer of coloured tiles, while windows are framed with sinister bone-shapes, and the blue and mauve tiled roof looks, some have suggested, like a dragon's back. The interior is just as impressive; the attic is a labyrinth of cool white arches and the roof is peppered with Gaudí's trademark mosaic chimneys. Entry is €16.50. 🚇 Drassanes, Map 4 C3 🏧

Casa Batlló at night

Casa Milà (La Pedrera)

93 484 59 00

C/ de Provença, 261-265   www.fundaciocaixacatalunya.org

Gaudí's creation was dismissively nicknamed 'la pedrera' (the quarry) on its opening by unimpressed locals. The name has stuck but attitudes have changed: it's now one of the city's main Unesco World Heritage sites. Inside, Fundació Caixa Catalunya hosts regular, free exhibitions. Admission to the main building costs €8 and includes access to a Gaudí exhibition in the attic, as well as a typically playful roof and a show-flat furnished in the *modernisme* style. ☒ Diagonal, Map 4 D1 🔟

Fundació Antoni Tàpies

93 487 03 15

C/ Aragó, 255   www.fundaciotapies.org

Antoni Tàpies is commonly regarded as Catalonia's greatest living artist. His challenging, enigmatic works draw loosely on abstract expressionism. You don't have to step inside to get a taste: the foundation is topped by the silver tangle of one of his wire sculptures. The building itself, by Lluís Domènech i Muntaner, is said to be Barcelona's first *modernisme* work. As well as housing the most complete collection of Tàpies's work, the building houses regular, normally excellent, touring exhibitions. Entry is €6. ☒ Passeig de Gràcia, Map 4 C3 🔟

Hospital de la Santa Creu i Sant Pau

93 256 25 04

Sant Antoni Maria Claret, 167-171   www.santpau.es

Built between 1902 and 1930 by master architect Lluís Domènech i Montaner, this still-functioning hospital is an elaborate fantasy of red-brick and coloured tiles, with echoes of Montaner's Palau de la Música (p.16). Like the Palau, it's a

La Sagrada Família remains a work in progress

Unesco World Heritage site. Luckily, there's no need to fake injury to visit: the public are free to wander the gardens and admire the various pavilions. There are also guided tours every morning. Phone ahead to book a place or visit www. rutadelmodernisme.com. 🚇 Hospital de Sant Pau, Map 1 D2

Temple Expiatori de la Sagrada Familia 93 207 30 31
C/ de Mallorca, 401 www.sagradafamilia.org
In a city full of stunning buildings, the Sagrada Familia is outstanding. Something akin to a giant fairytale sandcastle, it's Gaudí's masterpiece. Although Gaudí devoted himself to it for the last 14 years of his life, anarchists destroyed all his plans and models during the Civil War, and work wasn't resumed until the 50s. It's still very much under construction today, making it a lively cathedral to visit. Visitors can travel up the completed towers, watch the ongoing work and visit the basement museum, all for €8. 🚇 Sagrada Familia, Map 5 B2 15

If you only do one thing in...
Eixample

The Fundació Francisco Godia (93 272 31 80, Carrer Valencia 284, www.fundacionfgodia.org) is a charming place, highlighting Godia's eye for *modernisme* artists such as Santiago Rusiñol and Ramón Casas.

Best for:

Eating: Soft piano jazz, droll chatter and mouthwatering scents fill the air at Noti (p.197), a slick, sophisticated eatery.

Drinking: Get dolled up for an evening at the upmarket Buda Bar (p.200): this is where the beautiful people go to mingle with their own kind.

Shopping: Browse the exclusive designer boutiques on Passeig de Gràcia (p.138), then hotfoot it to the chain stores of Rambla de Catalunya.

Families: Kids will be especially drawn to the tombs and treasures of the Museu Egipci (93 488 01 88, Carrer València 284).

Outdoors: The gardens of the Hospital de Santa Pau i Santa Creu (p.92) are a rarity in this built-up *barri*.

Above Eixample

There's plenty to explore in the outlying districts, with quirky, charming Gràcia, wealthy Sarrià, and Camp Nou, the home of FCBarcelona.

Above the Avignuda Diagonal the city takes on several different characters, as it has grown to envelop smaller towns. There's Gràcia, the proudly alternative, villagey district that has a staggering 800 or more bars and a thriving cultural scene; Gaudí's stunning Park Güell (p.98) solidly wealthy Sarrià-Sant Gervasi; the hilltop church and funfair of Tibidabo (p.99); and spacious Les Corts, dominated by the FCBarcelona stadium, Nou Camp (p.98).

For **restaurants and bars** in the area, see p.202.
For **shopping**, see Carrer Verdi, p.139 Pedralbes Centre, p.147.

CosmoCaixa

C/ de Teodor Roviralta, 47-51

93 212 60 50
www.cosmocaixa.com

Barcelona's science museum is among the best in the city for kids, as it's designed for young, inquisitive minds. Interactive features guide the visitor towards discovering scientific principles for themselves. Highlights include a huge geological wall that's a cross-section of the world's rock formations, and the flooded forest (a reproduction of an Amazon rainforest inside a greenhouse), complete with wildlife, some of which can be handled. Entrance costs €3; there are supplements for some activities.

🚇 Vall d'Hebron

Park Güell's famous salamander

Nou Camp/Museu Barça

93 496 36 08

Av Arístides Maillol

www.fcbarcelona.cat

The museum is attached to the magnificent Nou Camp ('El Camp Nou', to locals) and houses memorabilia spanning the club's 100 plus years. There are trophies, shirts, photos, artefacts – even the boot worn by Ronald Koeman when he scored the winning goal in the 1992 European Cup final. Three audiovisual displays trace the club's origins and show footage of some of the best players. Museum entry and a tour of the stadium is €11 for adults. 🚇 Les Corts, Map 1 A1

Park Güell

93 413 24 00

C/ d'Olot and Av Coll del Portell

www.bcn.es/parcsijardins

Antoni Gaudí's fairytale playground is the city's most stunning park, offering panoramic city views and breathtaking decorative flourishes, including the iconic mosaic salamander. There's hardly a straight line in the place: everything curves or ripples, especially the multi-coloured benches that ring the central platform. Originally intended as a luxury housing estate, only two houses were ever built - Gaudí lived in one, now a museum – and the whole site was donated to the city in 1922. Admission is free. 🚇 Vallcarca, Map 1 D1

Pedralbes Monastery

93 203 92 82

Baixada del Monestir, 9

www.museuhistoria.bcn.es

This monastery of the Poor Clare Nuns is a beautiful building which, though open to visitors, remains a peaceful and dignified space. A recently widowed Gothic queen, Elisenda de Montcada, founded the order with her inheritance in 1327,

Tibidabo Amusement Park

and then joined it herself. It is a gorgeous example of Gothic architecture, and Elisenda lies in a superb marble tomb. Entrance is €5. 🚇 Reina Elisenda (FGC), Map 1 A1

Tibidabo Amusement Park

93 211 79 42
www.tibidabo.es

Pl de Tibidabo, 3-4

This is the oldest amusement park in Spain and second oldest in Europe. The Castle of Terror and the Big Dipper have been going for 100 years, and are quaint rather than terrifying. Prices are €22 for adults, €9 for kids. To get to the park from the Avinguda Tibidabo FCG, take the century-old tram, Tramvia Blau, up the hill, and then connect to the equally ancient art-deco funicular. 🚇 Av Tibidabo (FGC)

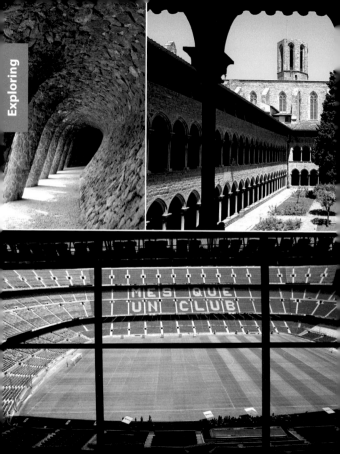

If you only do one thing in...
Above Eixample

For huge, well-presented collections of beautiful objects, the Ceramics Museum and Museum of Decorative Arts are hard to beat.

Best for...

Relaxation: For beauty treatments, massage and other forms of pampering, try Aqua Urban Spa (p.129).

Eating: Botafumeiro (p.203) has become wildly popular owing to its mind-blowing seafood and fish dishes.

Drinking: Roam the streets and plaças of Gràcia, especially in the summer months, when it's all about drinking alfresco and watching the world go by.

Outdoor: Head to the parc de la Collserola (www.parccollserola.net), the 8,000 hectares of nature above the Ronda de Dalt.

Families: The vivid, crazy gingerbread houses and hidden corners of Park Güell (p.98) are hugely appealing to kids.

Further Out

Escape the city limits to glimpse the seaside resorts, mountain ranges and historic towns of Catalonia.

If you're finding Barcelona's beaches a little crowded, a worthwhile alternative is taking a half-hour train ride to one of the city's satellite towns, such as Castelldefels, Mataró or Premià, where the wider, cleaner beaches have considerably more space to pitch a towel.

There are plenty of other reasons to head out of town: Catalonia's landscape encompasses mountain ranges as well as the stunning shoreline, while the region's historic wealth has created some beautiful towns and sites.

Montserrat

Catalonia's sacred mountain juts up from the surrounding plains in a dramatic formation of stone fingers. It's a stunning setting for the region's spiritual centre, the Monastery of Santa Maria de Montserrat (93 877 77 01, www.abadiamontserrat.net). The most visited section is the ornate 16th century basilica, where Catalan pilgrims queue for a glimpse of La Moreneta statue, the black Virgin Mary mysteriously discovered in a nearby cave in the Middle Ages. The cave where La Moreneta was discovered now has a small chapel, where pilgrims leave gifts in the hope that prayers will be answered: Barça FC scarves, learner driver plates and wedding veils line one wall.

In the main abbey complex, there's a large museum with an eclectic collection, comprising everything from Picasso and Caravaggio paintings to Egyptian mummies; there's also a visitor's centre, with a cafe and gift shop.

FCG trains run hourly from Plaça d'Espanya station to Aeri de Montserrat station, where there's a cable car service to the abbey, and then to Monistrol de Montserrat, where there's a rack railway.

Girona

This wealthy provincial capital gives a taste of how Barcelona's Barri Gòtic may have been 30 years ago. Rather than frenetic and lively, it's a tranquil place, with an immaculately-preserved Gothic quarter, a pretty river, overlooked by its cathedral (Plaça de la Catedral s/n), which perches on a hill at the city centre. Built between the 11th and 17th centuries, it is a beautiful mishmash of styles, and well worth the slog up the long stone staircase.

If you only have a day here, visit the Banys Àrabes (97 221 32 62, Carrer Ferran el Catòlic s/n), a 12th century bathhouse in the Moorish style, and the atmospheric Call district, which was home to one of Spain's biggest Jewish communities in the Middle Ages. There's a small museum on Girona's Jewish past (97 221 67 61, Carrer Força 8) housed in a lovely building.

The Girona Tourist Office (97 222 65 75, Rambla de la Llibertat 1, www.ajuntament.gi/turisme) can supply maps, leaflets and accommodation options. Renfe trains run from Passeig de Gràcia station to Girona roughly every hour; the journey takes around 90 minutes.

Sitges

The pretty, flirtatious seaside spot of Sitges has a long-held reputation as a party town. Once a peaceful fishing village, it was adored by Modernista artist Santiago Rusiñol and his set, and has been a favourite with artists and bohemian types. In the past few decades it's developed Spain's biggest gay scene, complete with an utterly fabulous carnival at Mardi Gras.

It's easy to see why people are drawn to the town. It has great beaches and disordered, picturesque, whitewashed houses, and a number of extravagant Modernista buildings. Rusiñol's home is now the beautiful Museu Cau Ferrat (93 894 03 64, Carrer Fonollar 8), and has a fine collection of works by the artist and his contemporaries.

The seafront has plenty of places for leisurely paella lunches, while the town centre is especially good at night, when it hums with gay and mixed bars and clubs.

The tourist information office (93 810 93 40, Carrer Sinia Morera 1) will help you with maps, brochures and accommodation bookings. Sitges is about an hour by train from Passeig de Gràcia, and trains leave every 20 minutes.

Tarragona

An hour south of Barcelona, stately Tarragona has a grand history. In Roman times, the city of Tarraco was the Empire's capital of its Spanish territories, and successive empires have left their traces around the magnificent Roman ruins.

The ruins themselves are impossible to miss: there's the impressive amphitheatre, picturesquely silhouetted against the Mediterranean, as well as three Roman towers, walls and the circus, all of which can be visited. The Museu Nacional Arqueològic (97 725 15 15, Avinguda Ramon i Cajal 76-78, www.mnat.es) has an excellent collection.

There's also a well-preserved medieval quarter, with Catalonia's largest cathedral (97 723 86 85, Plaça de la Seu), a stunning building dating back to the 12th century. Information on other museums and galleries, as well as maps, are available at the Tourist office (97 725 07 95, Carrer Major 39, www.turismetarragona.cat). Trains run from Estació de Sants and Passeig de Gràcia every hour, and take 75 minutes.

Figueres

The dandyish godfather of surrealism was from nearby fishing village Cadaqués, and spent much of his later life in this corner of Spain. The Teatre-Museu Dalí (97 267 75 00, Plaça Gala-Salvador Dalí 5, www.salvador-dali.org) was designed by the artist to showcase his own work. It is as outlandish and flamboyant as the creations it displays.

The round building is covered on the outside with sculpted bread rolls, and topped with large eggs. Inside it's more like a fairground tent than an art gallery, with whirring sculptures and artworks that demand you climb a ladder to view them.

There are other Dalí museums at his former house and studio in Port Lligat, and at Púbol, the castle he bought and transformed for his wife, Gala, but they are harder to reach from Barcelona (see website, above, for more details). To get to the Teatre-Museu, catch the Renfe train from Passeig de Gràcia to Figueres, then follow the signs.

Tour Operators

Find a boat or helicopter tour, or get the experts to show you the city up-close.

Barcelona Bus Turístic

93 285 38 32

Various Locations
www.barcelonaturisme.com

This is a comprehensive hop-on, hop-off tour bus service. There are three interconnecting routes covering most of the city: North, South and Forum. Each bus has a multi-lingual guide. A one-day adult ticket costs €19 (€23 for two days). Discount vouchers for some sights are included in the price. Tickets can be bought on board.

Barcelona Tours

93 317 64 54

Rda de la Universitat, 5
www.barcelonatours.es

This is the other major open-top bus tour, boasting 50 years experience. It runs in the same way as Turístic (see above), but with fewer stops (around 20), so it's often less crowded. It has an eight language audio guide. Price for the day is €20.

Scenic

93 225 22 30

C/ Balboa, 3
www.scenicbcn.com

Scenic provides guided tours of the city streets by bike, scooter (kick-scooters as opposed to the motorised variety) or roller-blade, as well as mountain bike trips into the hills and paint-balling excursions out in the sticks. Their HQ is in Barceloneta, from where they also run kayak tours and schooner trips around the harbour and out to sea.

Tour Operators

Bike Tours

Biciclot	93 221 97 78	www.biciclot.net
Classic Bikes	93 317 19 70	www.barcelonarentbikes.com
Fat Tire Bike Tours	93 301 36 12	www.fattirebiketoursbarcelona.com
Un Cotxe Menys	93 268 21 05	www.bicicletabarcelona.com

Boat Tours

Barcelona Orsom	93 221 82 83	www.barcelona-orsom.com
Las Golondrinas	93 442 31 06	www.lasgolondrinas.com

Food & Wine Tours

Smashed!	93 342 52 52	www.smashedtravel.com
Vinomadas	609 314 622	www.vinomadas.com

Helicopter Tours

CAT Helicòpters	93 224 07 10	www.cathelicopters.com

Other Tours

Julià Travel	934 815 449	na
BGB	932 682 422	www.bgb.es
Pullmantur	933 414 900	na

Rickshaw Tours

Trixi	93 455 58 87	www.trixi.com

Scooter Tours

Barcelona Scooter	93 285 38 32	www.barcelonaturisme.com

Walking Tours

APIT	93 319 84 16	www.apit-barcelona.org

Sports & Spas

Introduction

Barcelona leaves visitors with little time to feel bored. But do you want to lie back and be pampered, or get out and be active?

As you'd expect from a city that earned its stripes hosting the Olympic Games, Barcelona leaves sporting enthusiasts spoilt for choice. Of course, the climate helps: warm summers and mild, sunny winters make spending time outdoors a pleasure.

There's something on offer all year round. Yachting, windsurfing, kitesurfing and other watersports (p.118) on the Mediterranean are particularly popular in the breezy spring and autumn months, while there are also several good quality golf clubs (p.144) within easy reach of the city centre. Catalonia offers excellent rock climbing opportunities, with some great ranges close to Barcelona (p.112): the city itself also has several indoor climbing walls (p.112).

Between December and March, it's just about possible to go on day trips to the ski slopes at La Molina (97 289 20 31, www.lamolina.cat) and Vall de Núria (97 273 20 20, www.valldenuria.cat). A full day out, including passes, train tickets, and ski hire, can be had for under €100.

If you're determined not to let your gym rhythm slip while you're away, the basic, affordable municipal sports centres often welcome one-off visitors (generally €5 to €7). Although you won't get little niceties like towels, they often have swimming pools and saunas.

If you're more intent on spectating than participating, you're in good company. The city is fanatical about its football. Key FCBarcelona matches can set the rooftops ringing throughout the city with the shouts and cheers of support, and thousands flock to Camp Nou (p.98) for every home game. The city is also home to a number of other events and tournaments, and the Barcelona Grand Prix (see p.124), held each year, is only a short distance out of the city.

Not all Barcelona's activities are sporting however, there is also a range of cultural activities, from cookery courses to flamenco workshops, and many cultural centres offer intensive dance courses in July (see www.bcn.cat for details). Lifestyle Barcelona (93 270 20 48, www.lifestylebarcelona. com) organises a range of one-off sports and cultural events to keep you entertained.

The Spanish are increasingly enamoured with day spas (p.126), beauty treatments (p.127) and 'wellness' centres (p.130), so there is plenty of relaxation and pampering on offer. Most day spas can be visited without membership, for around €25 to €40 a day. Several of the top hotels have spa facilities that can also be visited for the day.

Regular beauty treatments, particularly waxing, manicures and pedicures, are common and regarded as a necessity rather than an indulgence, while treatments such as cellulite removal and even Botox are on the rise. Prices have become competitive, with leg waxing costing €15 and facials €20. There are beauty salons scattered liberally throughout town and many of the fancier hairdressers also offer basic treatments.

Activities

This is an active city with a climate that encourages sport, and there are dozens of ways to get sweaty.

Bowling

Bowling Pedralbes
Av Doctor Marañón, 11

93 333 03 52
www.bowlingpedralbes.com

Fourteen lanes of 10 pin bowling, plus foosball and snooker tables, make Bowling Pedralbes a good option for rainy-day entertainment. It's worth the trek (it's just behind the Camp Nou stadium) and is pretty affordable, with prices as low as €2 a game during the day on working days (costs increase to €4.75 a game for Saturday nights). Map 1 A1

Climbing

Climbat Barcelona
C/ del Moianès

93 432 99 08
www.climbat.com

An indoor climbing centre with an artificial wall (búlder), equipment hire, and shop. The centre offers courses and excursions to nearby climbs, normally at Montserrat, a fantastic range an hour out of town. One session costs €9 to €12. There are short courses for beginners (€35) that include two climbing sessions, footwear hire, and some teaching. In the summer, they also offer guided climbing tours around the region in English and Spanish. Espanya, Map 1 A2

La Fuixarda Montjuïc
Av de l'Estadi, 30-38

93 423 40 41
www.picornell.com

This is the largest urban climbing area in Europe and the most popular among climbers in Barcelona. It can become crowded, but with 150 routes there's usually space for everyone. The main climbing wall is lit until 23:00 every night. It's a friendly, sociable place where it's easy to find a climbing partner, and best of all, it's free. ⬡ Universitat, Map 6 A3 **1**

Cookery Classes

Cook and Taste
La Rambla, 58, 3a

93 302 13 20
www.cookandtaste.net

This school offers classes in traditional Catalan cuisine taught in English, French and Spanish. Half-day courses last three and a half hours and are run twice a day (12:00 and 18:00) from Monday to Sunday. Each session costs €50 including the class, a meal with Spanish wine and a booklet of translated recipes.
⬡ Liceu, Map 9 D2 **2**

Coquus
C/ de Ferrer de Blanes, 7

93 368 02 29
www.coquus.es

Offers classes in English, Spanish and German that explore typically Spanish and Catalan cuisine. Coquus uses fresh market ingredients, purchased on a tour of the market. The group makes its own tapas, which is then tasted and washed down with an excellent Rioja. It's particularly good if you want to learn cooking in Barcelona but just don't have the time for weekly class. ⬡ Diagonal, Map 2 D4 **3**

Golf

Masia Bach Golf Club
Sant Esteve Sesrovires

93 772 88 00
www.golfmasiabach.com

One of the more modern and challenging courses in the Barcelona region, Masia Bach is an 18 hole course located 25km from the city centre. There's also a nine hole course for less experienced players. Green fees for the 18 hole course are €75 on weekdays and €170 on weekends, public holidays and Fridays from 13:00 onwards.

Reial Club de Golf El Prat
Plans de Bonvilar

93 728 10 00
www.rcgep.com

This elite club boasts two meticulously maintained 18 hole, par 72 courses, a 30 minute drive from Barcelona. Reial allows non-members to play if they can show current membership to a golf club in their home country, or have a handicap officially validated by the governing golf body at home. Green fees cost €114 on weekdays and €228 on weekends.

Sant Cugat Golf Club
Sant Cugat

93 674 29 08
www.golfsantcugat.com

The oldest course in Catalonia, within easy reach of Barcelona, Sant Cugat prides itself on its history and the quality of the 18 hole, par three course. Green fees cost €65 on weekdays and €150 from Friday to Sunday and on holidays. If you're planning a game, you need to be able to show proof that you play golf; for example showing membership to a foreign club.

Gyms & Swimming Pools

Can Ricart
Sant Oleguer, 10

93 441 75 26
www.canricart.com

Can Ricart has an open-plan gym and a range of daily fitness classes. A large free weight and resistance area downstairs, with cardiovascular machines and exercise mats upstairs. There is a 25m indoor swimming pool and a small outdoor solarium. A spa pool with water jets and Jacuzzi is open too. Entry to the pool costs €10 per person.

Paral·lel, Map 9 A3 **4**

Club Natació Atlètic-Barceloneta
Pl del Mar, s/n

93 221 00 10
www.cnab.org

Set right on the beach, this club has all the usual gym and fitness facilities, along with ping pong. There are three large pools, Jacuzzis and masseurs. The club is clean and well-run, staff are helpful and members seem excruciatingly bronzed. Entry is €9.80 for adults. Barceloneta, Map 1 D1

Club Natació Catalunya
Pg Joan de Borbó, 93

93 213 43 44
www.cncat.org

This municipal fitness centre in Gràcia is a favourite among locals. It's particularly child friendly and hosts a number of activities for families. The main focus is on the indoor and outdoor pools, but other facilities include a gym, exercise rooms for fitness classes, solarium, sauna, climbing wall and squash courts. Entrance is €7.35. Mercat Nou, Map 11 F2 **5**

Hiking

Catalonia Adventures

93 890 45 14

Various Locations
www.cataloniaadventures.com

This English, Spanish and Catalan-speaking company organises guided trails in the Pyrenees, Aigüestortes, Montseny and Montserrat, finishing up with some tasty traditional grub in a local restaurant. You can also mix in canyoning, skydiving, climbing, bungee jumping, caving or mountain biking on longer trips.

Federació d'Entitats Excursionista de Catalunya

La Rambla 41, Ciutat Vella
www.feec.org

FEEC is an essential point of reference for information on trails and excursions. On its website, it lists hiking trails divided into three categories: *senders locals* (marked by green signs), *senders de petit recorregut* (yellow trails between 5km and 50km long) and *senders de gran recorregut* (red trails between 50km and 500km long). FEEC also organises group excursions. Call 93 412 07 77. Liceu, Map 9 C3 6

Follow The Baldie

617 039 956

Various Locations
www.followthebaldie.com

This small local company offers one-day hikes off-the-beaten-track, avoiding tourist hot spots. The experienced 'baldie' is a fountain of knowledge on local culture, biodiversity and celebrations, and speaks English, Dutch and Spanish. Most excursions include a visit to a local bar or restaurant, an isolated castle, a hidden cave or traditional village fiesta.

Horse Riding

Natural Hípic   609 438 080
Various Locations   www.naturalhipic.com

Natural Hípic's Three Breeze Ranch could be straight out of a
Wild West movie. The equestrian centre specialises in horse
breaking and western-style mounting, incorporating complex
horsemanship, reining techniques, trail, pole bending and
barrel racing. If you have experience in horse riding and want
to try something wild and adventurous, get in touch.

Escola Municipal d'Hipica La Foixarda 93 426 10 66
Av Montanyans 14-16, Montjuïc

This school is high up on Montjuïc, with stunning views of
the city. The school's facilities include three equestrian jump
circuits, one outdoor course, an indoor arena and a riding
school for all ages and abilities. Prices start from €15 per hour
for group lessons. The school itself doesn't have a website,
but you can find out more information by phone or through
www.picornell.com. ⊙ Espanya, Map 6 A2 **7**

Ice Skating

Gel Skating Club   93 245 28 00
C/ Roger de Flor, 168   www.skatingclub.cat

When the heat gets unbearable, one place you can chill is at
this ice rink in Eixample. Opening hours vary but it's usually
10:30 to 21:00, with a break for lunch. Entry is €13, including
skate and glove hire. ⊙ Verdaguer, Map 5 A3 **18**

Mountain Biking

Open Natura
646 962 121

Various Locations
www.opennatura.com

Open Natura organises weekend excursions around Catalonia for all ages and abilities. There are children's circuits (*circuit infantil*), intermediate circuits (*circuit intermig*) suitable for teenagers and adults who don't want to push themselves too hard, and long circuits (*circuit llarg*). Excursions cost between €14.50 and €21. 🚇 Sants Estació, Map 1 B2

Watersports

Centre Municipal de Vela
93 225 79 40

Moll de Gregal, s/n
www.velabarcelona.com

This centre offers windsurfing and sailing courses. These are good value and well taught. Windsurfing courses (€159 plus €25 signing-up fee) comprises of eight intensive hours of teaching either Monday to Thursday or over two weekends. Private lessons are available. 🚇 Llacuna, Map 14 D3 [8]

Canal Olímpic de Catalunya
93 664 57 73

Av Canal Olimpic, s/n
www.canalolimpic.com

This watersports centre in Castelldefels, constructed for the 1992 Olympics, offers eight to 10 hour courses in kayaking, windsurfing and canoeing. There is also a gym on-site which non-members can use. Canoes, kayaks, rowing boats, windsurfing boards and Optimists (little sailing boats) can be hired for €10 an hour.

Boats in Port Olímpic

Spectator Sports

Sport is never just a game in Barcelona: the city that houses Europe's biggest stadium takes competition very seriously indeed.

Basketball

Joventut de Badalona
C/ Ponent, 143-161

93 460 20 40
www.penya.com

Based just outside the city limits (but on the metro line 2), Joventut compete in Spanish basketball's top tier. During the 90s they chalked up two league titles and a European Cup. Nicknamed *La Penya*, they play in green and black at their home arena, the Palau Olímpic, so named for its hosting of the semi-legendary basketball matches of the 1992 games. Tickets are available via the club website. 🚇 Les Corts, Map 1 A1

FCBarcelona
Av Aristides Maillol

902 189 900
www.fcbarcelona.com

Spain's second most popular spectator sport has a top FCBarcelona-branded team that plays in the Palau Blaugrana (the 'blue and maroon palace'). Handball and rollerhockey teams also play in the maroon and blue strip, along with non-professional athletics, cycling, rugby, baseball, volleyball, field hockey, ice hockey and ice dance divisions. Located on the same site as the iconic Camp Nou stadium, Palau Blaugrana is home to regular basketball matches. 🚇 Les Corts, Map 1 A1

A poster for one of Barcelona's last *corridas*

Bullfighting

Plaza de Toros Monumental
Gran Via de les Corts, 749

93 245 58 02
www.torosbarcelona.com

Barcelona isn't mad about bullfighting (partly because of its consistent identification with Spain and Spanishness) and the city's last surviving bullring caters mostly to tourists and out-of-towners, with continual speculation about its imminent closure. For now though, bullfighting season is April to September and tickets start from €21, with shaded seats being more expensive than those in the sun. Tickets can be bought from the ticket booth at the ring, through ServiCaixa or from an outlet on Carrer Muntaner. 🚇 Glòries, Map 5 C4 9

Cycling

Escalada a Montjuïc
Montjuïc

915 400 841
www.rfec.com

Cycling has traditionally been one of the most popular sports in Spain and, although recent doping scandals have dampened enthusiasm, it remains a firm favourite in Catalonia. A stage of the Tour de France heads through the Pyrenees, and the Volta de Catalunya is a week-long annual event that draws a pool of the world's top riders to the region. For something in the city-centre though, the *Escalada a Montjuïc*, held each October, is one of the last of the European racing season. Held since 1965, it takes place over one day but is split into two stages: a 5km circuit followed by a 10km time trial up the slopes of Montjuïc.

Football

FCBarcelona
Camp Nou, Av Aristides Maillol

902 189 900
www.fcbarcelona.com

The home of FCBarcelona, Camp Nou, is a place of quasi-spiritual significance for Catalans. During the Franco years, support for the team was the only permitted outlet for Catalan nationalism. Watching a match here is an unforgettable experience, and doesn't have to cost the earth (although don't expect to get a seat for big matches like '*El Clasico*' with Real Madrid). Tickets can be bought from www.servicaixa.com. A Norman Foster-designed, Gaudí-inspired facelift will finish in 2011. Building should not affect games. 🚇 *Les Corts, Map 1 A1*

The magnificent Camp Nou

RCD Espanyol
93 292 77 00
Estadi Olímpic
www.rcdespanyol.com

Football and politics are never far apart in Catalonia. Just as FCBarcelona is inextricably linked to Catalan national pride (and even Catalan nationalism), supporting Espanyol still carries a whiff of loyalty to the Spanish flag. Although overshadowed by their bigger, richer rivals, Espanyol have enjoyed unprecedented success in recent times, winning the Spanish Cup in 2006 and reaching the UEFA Cup final in 2007. Match tickets are easy to get hold of, even for major games; try the Espanyol website. 🚇 Espanya, Map 1 A4

Motorsports

F1 Grand Prix
93 571 97 00
Circuits de Catalunya, Montmeló
www.circuitcat.com

Formula 1 racing has a long and chequered history in Barcelona, but with Spanish driver Fernando Alonso dividing public opinion and winning races, the Barcelona Grand Prix is a firm fixture on the F1 calendar. Held each May, the race takes place at Montmeló's Circuit de Catalunya, half an hour outside the city centre. The Circuit is superbly well-equipped, with 17 grandstands (three of which are under cover) and 25 giant screens to keep spectators up to pace with events. Tickets are available a year in advance and start at just over €100 for basic one-day admission to €500 for three days in the covered grandstand. For tickets, call the Circuit de Catalunya Ticket Hotline (93 571 97 71), or go through ServiCaixa.

Tennis

Tennis Vall d'Hebron
93 427 65 00
Av Vall d'Hebron
www.fctennis.org

Tennis has deep roots in Barcelona, and several schools and tournaments can be found. In 2007, elite women's tennis returned to Barcelona in the shape of the WTA Tour Barcelona KIA Tournament in June, and the intention is for it to become an annual summer event. Former champion and Barcelona legend, Arantxa Sánchez-Vicario, is in charge of the initiative and Vall d'Hebron certainly has the pedigree, having hosted the tennis events at the 1992 Olympics.

The Real Club de Tenis Barcelona
93 203 78 52
C/ Bosh i Gimpera, 5-13
www.rctb1899.es

The city's oldest tennis club plays host annually to the country's most prestigious tennis tournament, the *Trofeo Conde de Godó*, every April. This clay court competition was first played in 1953 and is now an ATP Gold tournament known as the Seat Open. Local hero, the Mallorcan Rafael Nadal, has won the last three tournaments, becoming the first player ever to do so. In the week preceding the main event, there is a seniors exhibition tournament. Tournament passes and tickets for the big games go on sale from late February but day passes in the early rounds can usually be bought during the tournament itself. Tickets are acquired through the club, by phone (902 332 211) or through ServiCaixa. 🚇 Palau Reial, Map 1 A1

Spas, Massage & Salons

Grooming is seen as a necessity rather than an extravagance, and pleasure hunters are spoiled for choice when it comes to being pampered in Barcelona.

Beauty Salons

Centre d'Estetica Groc

93 218 40 65
www.grocestetica.com

C/ Topazi, 9

This beauty salon in the centre of Gràcia has been in business since 1983, specialising in laser hair removal, facials, peeling and Botox treatments. Be prepared to pay a small fortune for treatments though, as this is not the place to come for a quick 10 minute wax. Spa, massage and nail treatments are also available. ⬛ Fontana, Map 2 E2 **10**

Centro de Terapias Naturales

93 313 29 75

C/ Maresme, 243

Located in Sant Martí, this centre focuses on natural, holistic treatments that draw on Asian and Indian influences, such as ayurvedic massages, as well as standard waxing and nail treatments. Acupuncture, reiki and homeopathic therapies are also available. This place has a more organic and natural philosophy towards beauty treatments. Contact the salon directly as prices vary depending on the length of time you need.

⬛ La Pau, Map 1 E1

Zensations

C/ Balmes, 44-46

93 272 20 23
www.holmesplace.es

Zensations lives up to its name; the place is calming and smells lovely. Their specialities are wine and chocolate therapy treatments which include massages, facials and full body moisturising treatments. These start from €45, whereas their standard facial and massage treatments start from €30. The site (part of Holmes Place) is reminiscent of a wood cabin in the mountains, allowing you to leave feeling warm and glowing. Bridal packages, multi-treatments, manicures, pedicures and tanning are also offered. 🚇 Universitat, Map 4 C3 🔟

Hair Salons

5º 1ª

Ronda Universitat, 20

93 412 51 62

This is a highly imaginative combined beauty salon and hairdresser. Unexpected massages, aromatherapy treatments and even the sound of the waves while you wait are all pleasant surprises. Hair is washed with deliciously scented shampoo and you get a head massage to finish. The basic women's cut costs from €22 and the mini beauty treatments are €1 per minute. 🚇 Universitat, Map 7 D1 🔢

Raffel Pages

Various Locations

93 215 14 69
www.raffelpages.com

This unisex chain salon is a household name in Barcelona, with over 20 branches in the city centre. Edgy cuts, razor-straight fringes and dramatic changes in image are specialities. Prices vary between salons, depending on location. Prices don't include conditioners, hair masks or any styling products that you wish to use on your hair, so watch out for the extra charges.

Salva G

93 302 69 86
C/ d'Avinyo 12
www.salvag.com

Standing out from the crowd is important at Salva G. Sharp layering, punk-esque mullets, off-centre fringes and anything that goes against the conventional is what this unisex salon aims for. Design is clearly thought out, right down to the last detail; multi-coloured lighting sets off the Redken products that the salon uses, and the coloured montages and leather sofas seem more lounge bar than hair salon. A cut and blow-dry costs €36, cuts for men cost €25. A good selection of highlights and lowlights are also available.

 Jaume I, Map 3 F3 13

Massage

Centro Kathmandu

680 210 596
Various Locations
www.tantriconepali.galeon.com

This centre specialises in oriental massages: ayurvedic, tantric, shiatsu, taoist and champi (upper body massage). Indian oils are used and oriental music plays in the backround. The ayurvedic massage (€75) covers the whole body and lasts one hour. It is more suitable for general relaxation and posture correction than for serious back problems. Shiatsu (€60 for 45 minutes) focuses on key pressure points and can be tailored to target specific back pains. Reservations are made by appointment only so call beforehand and the centre will reserve a treatment for you in either Universitat or Ciutat Vella.

Masajes A 1000
Various Locations

93 215 85 85
www.masajesa1000.net

Functioning on a no-booking system, Masajes a 1000 offers a walk-in and wait service for professionals of both sexes with little time to dedicate to beauty treatments. It is also one of the most reasonably priced options for massages, hair removal treatments and facials, but don't expect centres to be luxurious or queue-free, especially on Saturday mornings. Masajes a 1000 works on a ticket system: one ticket costs €4.80. Massages range from five minutes in a relaxation chair (one ticket) to 90 minutes on a massage bed (12 tickets). Foot massages cost two tickets.

Spas

Aqua Urban Spa
C/ Gran de Gràcia, 7

93 238 41 60
www.aqua-urbanspa.com

Treatments at this independent spa mix holistic trends, aromatherapy products and ancient Greek and Roman traditions. There are several different pools and jets, as well as a steam room, Roman sauna and Turkish bath. One spa session, usually lasting up to 90 minutes, costs €51. Packages are available combining massages and treatments with spa sessions. 🚇 Diagonal, Map 2 D4 14

Poliesportiu Marítim Talassoteràpia
93 224 04 40

Pg Marítim de la Barceloneta, 33-35   www.claror.org

This fresh seawater spa and swimming centre, part of the Marítim municipal sports centre, makes for a very affordable relaxation overlooking Barceloneta beach. During the week, the centre is blissfully tranquil. Beware however, of visiting at the weekends: the centre fills with excitable children. Weekday entry costs €14, and at weekends it's €16.50.

🚇 Barceloneta, Map 14 B2 18

Metropolitan Balmes
93 218 18 25

C/ Balmes, 215   www.clubmetropolitan.net

Although the compact, sleek spa zone of this wellness centre is attached to a members-only gym, non-members can enjoy the waterbeds, ice fountains, Jacuzzis and saunas for €30 a day, making this an affordable quick fix. There is also a full range of beauty and wellness treatments, including facials, massages and hot stone therapies. Call ahead to book.

🚇 Gràcia, Map 2 C3 15

Six Senses Spa
93 221 10 00

C/ Marina, 19-21   www.sixsenses.com

Located on two of the upper floors of the Hotel Arts, this exclusive relaxation facility includes saunas with stunning views over the Mediterranean, vitality pools and steam rooms, as well as offering über-luxurious pedicures, manicures, facials, massages and body wraps. Luxury like this doesn't come cheap (facials start at €115), but as a one-off treat it's unforgettable.

🚇 Llacuna, Map 14 B2 16

SpaciOmm

SpaciOmm, Hotel Omm
C/ Rosselló

93 445 40 00
www.hotelomm.es

SpaciOmm, the Zen-like spa area, is the newest addition to this ultra-modern hotel. Treatments have an eastern flavour: expect Tibetan head massages, shiatsu, and ayurvedic full-body massages and a host of other treatments which use natural plant-based oils. Aside from treatments, the spa has a small water circuit with a series of spa pools, Jacuzzis, plunge pools, Turkish bath and tatami cabin. There are also beauty treatments which combine ancient traditions with modern trends, such as the Inca ritual (€115), a holistic facial treatment (€70) and the four-handed massage.

🚇 Diagonal, Map 4 D1 17

Shopping

Shopping Barcelona

Whatever your budget, Barcelona has shopping opportunities galore. The only question is how you'll get it all home.

Spending money is a pleasure in compact, trend-conscious Barcelona: shops are handily clustered together so browsing independent boutiques, market stalls, high street brands or haute couture is a breeze. Whether you're after the latest clothing, local handicrafts or lavish coffee table tomes, there's a shopping experience for you. Throughout Ciutat Vella and Gràcia, little independently owned shops are the norm for design items, books, delicatessens, crafts, pottery and accessories such as leather goods. There are also regular temporary markets specialising in second-hand books, artesanal foods, handicrafts and even Christmas goods; these are organised most often in the Barri Gòtic (see Hotspots, p.136).

The local fashion scene is particularly indie in tone, producing quirky, funky designs. A number of fairs, markets and boutiques support local designers (see Where To Go For…, p.148). Head to Born and Gràcia for some of the most cutting-edge ideas (see Hotspots, p.136).

There's also a number of shopping malls and streets where the usual chain stores can be found. They're always joined by the biggest Spanish brands, which are rapidly conquering high streets globally. Clothing sold here is often considerably cheaper than in the same stores elsewhere, with the discounts on Spanish brands like Zara (p.136) and Mango (p.136) especially notable. Sales twice a year, in July and January, make prices even more tempting.

The main shopping malls are slightly outside the city centre, but they aim to make the journey worthwhile, with ice-cream stalls, food courts, cinemas and bowling. Meanwhile, in the city centre, Portal de l'Àngel and Rambla de Catalunya have the most comprehensive collections (see Hotspots, p.136). For the convenience of having everything under one roof, the Spanish institution El Corte Inglés (p.142) is the nation's leading department store, stocking everything from stationery to stereos.

For more upmarket fashion and other desirables, the genteel Eixample district is very promising, although the prices can be very high (see Hotspots, p.136).

Barcelona's vibrant craft scene has had a big impact, and there are many shops and galleries, particularly in Raval and Gràcia (see Hotspots, p.136). A bit of digging can unearth beautiful locally made jewellery or original artworks. Many of the souvenirs on sale are considerably classier than they tend to be in other cities (see Where To Go For… p.148). The museum shops are great places to pick up gifts and souvenirs, and also have very comprehensive book sections (p.92).

Opening Hours

Shops tend to close on Sundays. Otherwise, typical opening hours are 10:00 to 20:00 or 21:00. Smaller shops often close between 14:00 and 17:00, and for several weeks of August. Market stalls are generally open from 08:00 to 14:00.

Hotspots

Pick your route: shopping in Barcelona can lead you through some of the city's quirkiest corners and most chi-chi streets.

Avinguda Portal de l'Angel

This is a broad and hugely popular pedestrian strip, topped by the mammoth department El Corte Inglés that sits squarely on Plaça de Catalunya and boasts a slightly smaller branch of the store half-way down. Flanked by dozens of high-street fashion labels (see Where To Go For… p.148), Portal de l'Angel is the place to go if you want to blend in with the crowd (in every sense) rather than stand out from it. It's to be avoided at all costs on Saturday afternoons, but on weekdays it can offer relaxing and comfortable conditions for a decent comb through the sartorial delights of Zara, Mango, Bershka, Massimo Dutti et al. Shoe shops are also in abundance. Head off the main drag and into the surrounding streets for more youthful clothing and accessories.

Market stalls at the top end are often quite good for leather goods or Spanish pottery, and sometimes there are also bric-a-brac or seasonal markets in the large square at the bottom, outside the Cathedral. Map 7 F3 **1**

Barri Gòtic

The labyrinth of narrow streets that spider their way around Plaça Sant Jaume are a hectic but exhilarating jumble of modernity and tradition. This is the place to come for anything from antique lace to handmade chocolates, and there are dozens of colourful, funky clothing and accessory boutiques bringing the tone bang up to date. Shops stock everything from handmade candles and traditionally made, leather-bound notebooks to locally made silver jewellery and young, local fashion designs. The trick is to get lost and see what hidden gems you stumble across.

Carrer Banys Nous is particularly good for poking around in dusty little antiques shops, and has tiny places dedicated to vintage stamp and poster collectors. Oddly enough, they seem to sit quite comfortably alongside a thriving little community of bizarre alternative fashion shops such as Tomate and Glint.

Not too far away, on the other side of Carrer Ferran, is Carrer d'Avinyó, a long, narrow street that has become a favourite for young, fashion-conscious shoppers looking for something a little more cutting-edge, due to its cluster of independent boutiques. Carrer Ferran itself has a couple of good souvenir and pottery shops, as well as branches of two of the more important names in Barcelona's fashion world: the colourful, upmarket label Custo and eclectic, streetwise Desigual. Map 9 F2 ◪

MACBA Area, Raval

Ravalejar ('to ravalise') was an idea first introduced by a Catalan artist with a vision of a regenerated Raval. The once rough barrio has been undergoing something of a transformation in the past decade. These days, you're just as likely to head there for the perfect party dress as you are for a tattoo or septum piercing. The upper part of the area, around the MACBA, has become extremely trendy, with new shops, bars and cafes popping up all the time, while the lower area, around Carrer Nou de la Rambla, remains a little *chungo* (seedy).

Head to the streets around Carrer Doctor Dou for design-oriented places such as Ras, a gallery and bookshop, and boutique Dou16, which aims to nurture local fashion talent. The MACBA patio's enduring popularity with skateboarders means that the area has also been a natural choice for streetwear, trainer specialists and skate brands, while Carrer Bonsuccès is good for music shops. Map 7 C3 🖪

Carrer Rec, Born

The dense network of quaint little streets makes it a highly enjoyable place to spend lots of money. And the little boutiques that line these streets tend to be heartbreakingly expensive, stocking carefully chosen capsule ranges of clothing by Catalan and international designers. The shoe and accessory shops that are scattered among the boutiques and bars are similarly filled with desirable goodies. The look is one of trendy elegance; head to BoBa to get the picture. The area also has some good streetwear, with dedicated Carhartt, Pepe Jeans and Gas Jeans shops in the streets near to Carrer Rec, as well as local streetwear shop McQuinn. Check out nearby Sant Pere for slightly cheaper shops. Map 10 D3 🖪

Passeig de Gràcia, Eixample

The elegant avenue that runs up through the city is a fashionista's wish list of high-fashion names, with labels such as Chanel, Dolce & Gabbana and Burberry selling high-end fashion and accessories in atmospheres of supreme reverence. Spanish high fashion is represented too, with Loewe, Antonio Miro and Purificación Garcia also having large boutiques here. Local institution Santa Eulàlia stocks further couture labels, while yet more designers have branches clustered on the Diagonal around the top of Passeig de Gràcia.

High-street fashion has been gradually elbowing its way in along Passeig de Gràcia, with Benetton, Zara, H&M and Levi's holding their heads high among the haughty labels. There's a bigger variety of chain-stores along Rambla de Catalunya, which runs parallel. The streets branching off from Passeig de Gràcia offer some very genteel fashion and home furnishing shops. The closer to Diagonal you get, the smarter they become. 🚇 Passeig de Gràcia, Map 4 D3 🔄

Carrer Verdi, Gràcia

The boho yet deeply traditional neighbourhood of Gràcia is great for browsing boutiques, with hip little places clustered between the restaurants and bars of Carrer Verdi and around. Head for the chic Suite (p.149) for exquisite pieces by up-and-coming local talent, or Red Market for great trainers and sportswear at its most cutting-edge and achingly hip. There's classic menswear at century-old tailor's Camisería Pons, which also stocks local designers. Shoe and accessories shops are similarly small and funky. Món de Mones is a magpie's dream of dangly, sparkly little trinkets and more grown-up jewellery, while several of the local shoe shops sell brands such as Rocket Dog and Vialis. 🚇 Passeig de Gràcia, Map 1 C1

Markets

It may not be the quickest way to shop, but you can learn a lot about the city from a trip through its markets.

La Boqueria

93 318 25 84

La Rambla, 89

Barcelona's biggest market lies right on La Rambla. It can get very crowded in peak seasons, with everybody trying to get the same photo of perfectly stacked fruit, and locals trying to get their shopping done. The central section, with its huge spreads of fish and seafood on crushed ice, are especially mind boggling. Elsewhere, the jumble of charcuterie stands, cheese counters, spice stalls, butchers and other specialists makes for the city's best shopping experience. It's not for the faint hearted: this is a real, working food market, and it's perfectly normal to see things such as sheets of tripe, and whole skinned rabbits. There are also places specialising in high-quality Spanish wines and olive oils. Liceu, Map 9 D1

Fira de Bellcaire

93 246 30 30

Pl Glòries Catalanes, 8

Fira de Bellcaire, commonly known as Encants Vells (Old Charms), is the oldest flea market in Barcelona. Half an hour's rummaging will unearth washing machines, hairdryers, shoes, African furniture, Moroccan carpets, stolen mobile phones and emptied leather wallets. Mind your own wallet as you're walking around, as the place is a prime target for pickpockets. Encants Vells is not organised, clothes are left in piles on the ground, furniture spills out from under the stalls and toiletries overflow from their containers. However, if you want to find a real bargain, this is the place. You may have to trawl through a lot of tat, but when you do find something desirable, you can be sure that it will be dirt cheap. Open all day Monday, Wednesday, Friday and Saturday. 🚇 Glòries, Map 11 E4 A3 **7**

Mercat Sant Antoni   93 423 42 87
Comte d'Urgell, 1
If you're after an unvarnished market experience, Mercat Sant Antoni might be it. Throughout the week (closed on Mondays) clothing and second-hand bookstalls can be found here. There are also some slightly shabby stalls selling CDs, electrical accessories, books and trinkets of no practical use, all sold in an atmosphere of relaxed amicability. On Sunday mornings however, the market takes on a rather special, musty appeal, as the market hosts a weekly second-hand book and comic fair (08:00 to 14:00). 🚇 Sant Antoni, Map 6 F2 **8**

Mercat de Santa Caterina   93 319 57 40
Av Francesc Cambó, 16
This recently refurbished market in the Barri Gòtic offers a more relaxed ambiance than La Boqueria, with stalls selling high-quality olive oils, meats, cheeses, fish and vegetables. It has a decidedly fancy tone, partly due to its recent facelift: it is now housed under a spectacular multi-coloured, undulating roof designed by Enric Miralles. The crafty lighting allows shafts of sunshine to illuminate your prospective purchases appetisingly. 🚇 Jaume I, Map 10 C1

Shopping Malls

Apart from the kooky boutiques and meandering alleys, Barcelona has some mammoth shrines to shopping.

Bulevard Rosa

93 215 83 31
www.bulevardrosa.com

Pg de Gràcia, 51-57

Bulevard Rosa differs from other malls. Being smaller, it attracts more boutique-style shops and manages to maintain a more sophisticated image, despite the extremely low ceilings and dodgy overall decor. You will not find large high street or department stores here, nor will you find the bargain prices they offer. Instead, the mall focuses on speciality boutiques, local designers and high-quality, highly traditional children's garments. Despite this, Bulevard Rosa is not a child-friendly zone: there are no children's facilities, and shoppers tend towards yummy mummies who have left their little dears with the nanny. Its great location, and entrances on both Passeig de Gràcia and Rambla de Catalunya, is one of its main draws. Passeig de Gràcia, Map 4 D3

El Corte Inglés

902 22 44 11
www.elcorteingles.es

Various Locations

Department stores aren't hugely popular in Spain, apart from El Corte Inglés, which dominates city centres across the country with its landmark buildings and exhaustive stock. There are a number of megastores in Barcelona, including the absolutely huge one that occupies one side of Plaça de

Catalunya, and another half-way down Avinguda Portal de l'Àngel (p.136). Between these two central branches, they've got leather goods, cosmetics, men's, women's and children's fashion, home furnishings, music, sports gear, pet care, music and entertainment, computers and a travel agency. The Plaça de Catalunya branch also has a fab, if pricey, supermarket in the basement. Map 8 A2 **10**

Diagonal Mar

Av Diagonal, 3

90 253 03 00
www.diagonalmar.com

This spacious mall has a distinctly airy ambience, helped perhaps by its seaside setting. Its best feature is the terrace, filled with cafes, restaurants, tapas bars and icecream parlours. The hypermarket giant Alcampo, FNAC and high-street favourites Mango, Zara and H&M are present, as are all the other big brands of fashion, underwear, and cosmetics. There are plenty of family oriented activities such as a bowling alley, concerts and children's entertainment every Sunday at 12:30. If you can't face the city-centre scrums, or have your own car, Diagonal Mar makes a great alternative to Avinguda Portal de l'Angel (p.136). Maresme Fòrum, Map 1 F3

El Triangle

Pl Catalunya, 1-4

93 318 01 08
www.eltriangle.es

Entertainment and electronics giant FNAC and British home furnishings store Habitat dominate this mini mall, which leads onto Plaça de Catalunya. The presence of these giants threatens to dwarf the smaller jewellery and cosmetics stores – although Sephora, the deceptively large, *Alice in*

Wonderland themed cosmetics emporium, manages to hold its own. Calvin Klein Lingerie distracts the gaze of determined shoppers, as does the icecream parlour opposite. There's a string of familiar names along its Carrer Pelayo side, including Levi's and Accessorize. El Triangle's best feature is its central location, a stone's throw from La Rambla, making it particularly useful as a bolt-hole on those city-centre afternoons when it's too hot to function without some serious air conditioning. 🚇 Catalunya, Map 7 E2 **11**

Gran Via 2
Av Gran Via

90 230 14 44
www.granvia2.com

One of the biggest and busiest of Barcelona's malls, this complex has three floors and 180 shops dedicated to clothing, music, jewellery, books, technology and shoes. The children's facilities are more expansive than in other malls, with play areas both inside and out. Parking is not usually a problem as there are 3,400 spaces, each with three hours of free parking. The mall is well-serviced by several train and bus routes; the most direct and frequent buses leave from Plaça d'Espanya.

L'Illa Diagonal
Av Diagonal, 545-557

93 444 00 00
www.lilla.com

'The Island' is the work of architects Rafael Moneo and Manuel de Solà-Morales, whose design was inspired by the Rockefeller Center in New York. The €240 million project would seem rather outlandish if it weren't for the property values of the surrounding suburbs. The upmarket mall is

home to a branch of French entertainment giant FNAC, as well as El Corte Inglés, Diesel, Hermès, high-street favourites like Zara and Adolfo Domínguez, and sports store Decathlon.

🚇 Maria Cristina Map 1 B1

La Roca Village

93 842 39 00
www.larocavillage.com

La Roca del Vallés

This kitsch collection of faux-village buildings, is home to a surprisingly upmarket selection of labels, just half an hour's driving distance from the city centre. The trek is worthwhile though, considering the bargain prices on Burberry, Diesel, Tommy Hilfiger, Calvin Klein, and many others. There's also an ample selection of shoe sellers, beauty and accessories shops and several bargain-filled homeware stores, for those with extra space in their suitcases. Four buses a day connect La Roca to Barcelona's Fabra i Puig bus station in around 30 minutes. On the Renfe train, go from Barcelona Sants Station to Granollers Centre Station, where you can catch a special La Roca bus. If driving, it's exit 12 (marked 'Cardedeu') of the AP7 motorway.

Les Glòries

93 486 04 04
www.lesglories.com

Av Diagonal, 208

Despite its rather gaudy early 90s decor, Les Glòries is one of the most pleasant malls to shop in, due to its open spaces, alfresco cafes and relaxed atmosphere. A central square acts as a social hub, surrounded by cafes, restaurants and fastfood chains. There are over 220 shops, and a seven screen cinema that shows films dubbed into Spanish. Children's play areas and a free pram-lending service make for an enjoyable family experience. In the evening, you have a fantastic view of the brightly lit Torre Agbar, which stands just across the road from the mall. 🚇 Poblenou, Map 1 E3

Maremagnum

93 225 81 00
Moll d'Espanya
www.maremagnum.es

Maremagnum has recently undergone something of a makeover, replacing some rather tacky bars and clubs with upmarket stores such as Calvin Klein and Adolfo Dominguez. Even so, terrace bars and clubs remain, as does the large Miramax cinema. Mainstream high street stores are punctuated by boutiques and new designer outlets. The centre is child friendly, with sweet shops, a play area and children's clothing. There are several eateries with terraces that overlook the port. 🚇 Drassanes, Map 11 E4 **12**

Pedralbes Centre

93 410 68 21
Av Diagonal, 609-615
www.pedralbescentre.com

When this shopping mall opened in 1989, the objective was to make it exclusive. Space was offered to prestigious national and international establishments, curtailing the involvement of high street chains. There are 74 establishments in the mall, many of which are Catalan designers, such as Samblancat and Lluis Guirau. Sophisticated architecture and design make it a popular venue for catwalk presentations of new fashions. In the winter months, an ice rink is installed.

🚇 Maria Cristina, Map 1 A1

Beachwear

Sports shops and lingerie stores stock beachwear year-round. All the big surf labels have outlets, with Quiksilver a safe bet in terms of style and quality, however this comes at a price. Bikinis and board shorts here can cost as much as €80, which may seem expensive, but you're paying for quality material designed to withstand wear and tear.

For affordable, trendy beachwear, head to high street shops such as Bershka and H&M where you can usually pick up a bikini for under €10. The hosiery chain Calzedonia and lingerie chains Women'secret and Oysho all have generous selection of colourful bikinis at reasonable prices.

Bershka	93 302 01 04	www.bershka.es
Calzedonia	93 444 00 52	www.calzedonia.it
Oysho	93 488 36 09	www.oysho.es
Quiksilver	93 552 56 06	www.quiksilver.com
Women'secret	93 412 70 19	www.womensecret.com

Books

There are a number of English-language booksellers in the city, and some of the bigger Spanish bookshops (such as La Central and Casa del Llibre) also have a small English-language section. Hibernian, a new and second-hand bookseller in Gràcia, offers great browsing opportunities, while BCN Books has a good selection of novels. Altaïr specialises in travel, with a particularly comprehensive stock on Catalonia. Laie Pau Clan is good for art, design and history, with many titles in English. It also stocks poetry and novels.

Altaïr	93 342 71 71	www.altair.es
BCN Books	93 457 76 92	www.bcnbooks.com
Casa del Llibre	902 026 427	www.casadellibro.com
Hibernian Books	93 217 47 96	www.hibernian-books.com
La Central	93 487 50 18	www.lacentral.com
Laie Pau Claris	93 318 17 39	www.laie.es

Catalan Fashion

Head to Desigual for bold patterns and asymmetric cuts at high-street prices, or Custo if you're willing to part with some serious wedge on a T-shirt of cartoonish colourfulness. For something a little more indie, the chic little boutiques BoBa, Comité Shop and Dou16 all specialise in pieces by emerging local designers, as does Suite in Gràcia. Altogether more sober in tone, Catalonia's designer-in-chief remains Antonio Miro, whose well-cut men's suits and shirts and classic womenswear are worth every cent.

Antonio Miro	93 487 06 70	www.antoniomiro.es
BoBa	93 310 67 43	www.boba.es
Comité Shop	93 317 68 83	www.comitebarcelona.com
Custo Barcelona	93 342 66 98	www.custo-barcelona.com
Desigual	93 310 30 15	www.desigual.com
Dou 16	93 318 99 47	www.dou16.com
Suite	93 210 02 47	na

Designer Labels

Dolce & Gabbana, Armani, Dior, Max-Mara, Yves Saint
Laurent and Chanel all have their own boutiques on Passeig
de Gràcia, while Donna Karan and Gucci are nearby on the
Diagona. However, a couple of long-established independent
boutiques have achieved a semi-mythical status in the
city's shopping circles. Fashion junkies should attempt the
pilgrimage to both Santa Eulalia (which has been dressing
Barcelona's richest shoulders since 1843) and Jean-Pierre Bua.
Between them, they stock labels such as Balençiaga, Stella
McCartney, Marc Jacobs, Temperley, Matthew Williamson and
Alexander McQueen.

Armani Collezione	93 487 95 44	www.giorgioarmani.com
Burberry	93 215 81 04	www.burberry.com
Carolina Herrera	93 272 15 84	www.carolinaherrera.com
Chanel	93 488 29 23	www.chanel.es
Dolce & Gabbana	93 467 22 56	www.dolcegabbana.it
Donna Karan	93 414 12 00	www.donnakaran.com
Gucci	93 416 06 20	www.gucci.com
Jean-Pierre Bua	93 439 71 00	www.jeanpierrebua.com
Santa Eulalia	93 215 06 74	www.santaeulalia.com
Yves Saint Laurent	93 200 39 55	www.ysl.com

Gifts & Souvenirs

The streets around La Rambla and Sagrada Familia are
full of places to buy oversized Mexican hats and synthetic

FCBarça-themed underpants, but the Barri Gòtic also has plenty of places to find rather more stylish souvenirs. The museum shops also stock tasteful city-themed pieces; La Pedrera (p.92) and the Museu d'Història de la Ciutat (p.66) are worth a look.

Head to Carrers Ferran and Escudellers for simple handmade ceramics, or nearby Baixada de la Llibreteria for Cereria Subirà, a lovely candle shop (93 315 26 06).

Gourmet Food

Conveniently for visitors wanting to take the taste of holidays home, the Spanish are ingenious when it comes to making delicious things in jars, tins, and other durable packaging. Many stalls in the Boqueria and delicatessens can also vacuum-pack cured meats like jamón and chorizo, making them safe for travel. For a huge selection of olives, gourmet tinned fish, olive oils, biscuits and other treats, and a small deli counter with vacuum-packing, head to Colmado Quilez on the Rambla de Catalunya. Mind-blowingly beautiful handmade chocolates can be found at Patisseries Mauri, on the same street. If it's stuff from home you're after, you might find it in the international section of El Corte Inglés's food hall, or at DeliShop.

Colmado Quilez	93 215 87 85	www.lafuente.es
Corte Inglés	93 306 38 00	www.corteingles.es
DeliShop	93 215 15 46	www.delishop.es
Pastisseries Mauri	93 215 81 46	www.pasteleriasmauri.com

Wine

Spanish wines have gained some serious respect in the past five years. Catalonia has many vineyards and heavyweight producers, including Torres, which produces drinkable supermarket reds and exceptional vintages. Wines are cheap too, and bodegas are often able to arrange shipping for cases. Shopkeepers are usually very happy to offer advice.

Mas Bacus	93 453 43 58	na
Torres	93 317 32 34	www.torres.es
Vila Viniteca	93 327 77 77	www.vilaviniteca.es

Shoes

Those with a shoe fetish will be in seventh heaven in Barcelona. Styles range from vampy stiletto boots to colourful Camper shoes, and they're cheap too; expect to pay €50 to €60 for decent leather shoes. If Campers are too clumpy, look out for Vialis. These elegant but funky shoes come in some interesting colours and are widely available. The main Spanish shoe chains Vogue, Tascón and RoyAlty, have branches across town. Head to the streets around MACBA for trainers.

Camper	93 217 2384	www.camper.com
El Corte Inglés	901 122 122	www.elcorteingles.es
RoyAlty	93 209 51 32	www.royalty.es
Tascon	93 487 44 47	www.tascon.es
Vogue	93 301 90 35	www.voguelv.com

Going Out

Street Life

Barcelona is a city that starts its socialising late, and rolls on past dawn, every night of the week.

Drinking

From glitzy cocktail bars to eclectic, cheerfully scruffy little dives, Barcelona is well served for drinking establishments. Catalans don't tend to drink to get drunk: instead, the alcohol is a supplement to long and involved conversations or fervent dancing. Because of this, bars are less rowdy than they can be in the UK or Australia. Although they're often lively and crammed, it's very rare to see fights break out. Bars tend to cluster together in broadly similar types – see each area's write-up for the type of place to expect.

Evenings out typically start late (many bars don't get busy until midnight) and go on until the early hours and often stay open until 02:00 or 03:00 at weekends. However, cafes also serve alcohol, and whiling away an afternoon by slowly sipping beers on the sunny terrace of a cafe is one of the quintessential Catalan pleasures.

Table service is the norm: just grab a seat and someone will come and take your order – at busy times you may have to be quite assertive to get the waiter's attention, though. In most places, you pay at the end of the evening rather than after each round. Drinks can be very affordable – expect to pay €2 to €3 for a Spanish brand of beer or perfectly drinkable glass of wine, although mixed drinks are pricier (€7 to €8).

Spirits are free-poured, which can lead to ferociously strong drinks if the barman's in the mood. Cocktails aren't really a Barcelona tradition and can take ages to be made; caipirinhas and mojitos can be particularly variable. However, a growing number of funky cocktail lounges are currently raising the standard (see Venue Directory p.160).

Dining Out

Diners are spoilt for choice in Barcelona: the city has kebab shops, Michelin-starred restaurants, and plenty in between. Local Catalan cuisine is enjoying something of a 'moment' right now. In addition to scores of traditional Catalan eateries, the city also has a clique of highly skilled experimental chefs, led by far-out super-chef Ferran Adrià. Many of them have ultra-exclusive restaurants in Barcelona, such as Sergi Arola's Restaurante Arola (p.182) in the Hotel Arts.

There's as much seafood as you'd expect from a city this close to the Mediterranean, and plenty of it is very good indeed (see Venue Directory, p.160 for restaurants). There are dozens of upmarket, linen-tableclothed places that specialise in fish, paellas and mariscs (seafood), but there are also raucous little tapas bars where you pull up a stool at the bar and tuck into tiny plates of seafood so fresh it's practically twitching, patatas bravas (potatoes with paprika and garlic sauces), jamón (cured ham), and other morsels.

The international scene has recently improved, with a new generation of designer Indian, Thai, Turkish and Chinese restaurants appearing. Further down the price scale, the choices range from Ethiopian to Iraqi, and there are plenty of South American places that cater to the city's sizable Latin community.

Surprisingly for a city with so few Japanese residents, there's a myriad of sushi restaurants. But, the standard at many of these is pretty average.

Eating out doesn't have to be expensive: a set lunch menu (*menú del dia*) in a local restaurant will set you back €8 to €10, and supper in a decent restaurant can be had for €30 per head (including wine). Lunch is generally between 14:00 and 17:00, and if you arrive at 13:30 you can usually be sure of a decent table.

Restaurants tend to open at 20:00, but nobody eats much before 21:30; they'll stay open until around 01:00. Many restaurants are closed on Mondays and for a couple of weeks in August.

Tipping

Tipping isn't obligatory, but it's certainly appreciated: barmen, waiters and taxi drivers are all paid a decent amount, but a little extra is always welcome. If locals tip at all, they leave small change or round up to the nearest note. Don't feel under any pressure to cough up after receiving bad service though.

Tips tend to be modest, a few coins after coffee and drinks should be fine, and a couple of euros or the change from a note is acceptable in most restaurants. A word of warning, though: tips added to credit card bills tend to be divided by the staff, or even pocketed by the management.

Gay & Lesbian

Barcelona is a very tolerant place; few eyebrows are raised at men holding hands in the street and gay marriage has been legal in Spain since 2005. There's an open gay and lesbian scene, with several bars and clubs clustered together in a quadrant of the Eixample dubbed 'Gaixample'. Outside of the Gaixample, there's not much distinction between gay and straight establishments: most gay bars and cafés are open to straight clientele, while there are a number of straight bars that attract a sizeable gay crowd. Mainstream clubs often also run gay nights, such as Gay T Dance at Apolo (p.191).

Nightclubs

Authorities have cracked down on Ciutat Vella clubs, meaning that most of the city's clubbing destinations are in the outlying areas. Those that have survived, like Moog, (p.191) tend to be small, hip and intense. Bigger crowds head to the huge places in the suburbs, such as Razzmatazz (p.209) in Poblenou. Clubs don't start to fill up until 02:00 and they stay lively until dawn. Entry is typically €10 to €15.

The Yellow Star

This pretty yellow star highlights places that deserve some extra praise. It could be the atmosphere, the food, the cocktails, the music or the crowd – but whatever the reason, any review that you see with the star attached is somewhere that is a little bit special.

Venue Directory

Eating and drinking; the city's favourite hobbies

TAPAS

OQUETAS CASERAS
HOMEMADE CROQUETTES

HIPIRONES FRITOS
FRIED SMALL SQUIDS

AMARES A LA ROMANA
SQUIDS TO THE ROMAN

LPO A LA GALLEGA
OCTOPUS "GALLEGA" STYLE

ATATAS BRAVAS
POTATOES "BRAVAS"

AMBAS AL AJILLO
SHRIMPS TO THE CHOPPED GARLIC

MBAS A LA GABARDINA
SHRIMPS TO THE GABARDINE

EJILLONES AL GUSTO
MUSSELS TO THE TASTE

NGOSTINOS COCIDOS
COOKED PRAWNS

CHORICITOS

Barri Gòtic

Barri Gòtic is proof that some things just get better with age. It takes in the length of La Rambla, a mass of historic buildings, and some fine bars.

La Rambla is lined with overpriced restaurants squarely aimed at the tourist market, but elsewhere in the district are a multitude of decent eateries, with some good international food and some outstanding Catalan restaurants. The area is crammed with bars: if the Irish pubs of Carrer Ferran don't appeal, head to Carrer Ample and the streets around for hidden drinking delights.

Also In The Area

If you chose to drink on La Rambla, it might as well be in the splendid cafe of the Teatre Liceu (p.210), Café de l'Opera (93 317 75 85, La Rambla 74), a dusty but grand place that has remained untouched for decades. Another popular spot right in the thick of things is Café Zurich (93 317 91 53, Plaça de Catalunya 1). It is at the corner of the El Triangle shopping centre, and has a carefully preserved century-old interior.

For a taste of deeply traditional drinking and dining, Bodega La Plata (93 315 10 09, Carrer Mercè 28) has towers of dusty wine barrels and is good for tapas. In the same area, the slinky lounge bar Dusk (93 315 25 42, Carrer Mercè 23) serves up an imaginative supper menu, and also has a small Irish-style bar area, with screens showing live matches. The lively cocktail bar Maria Mulata (93 295 55 84, Carrer Mercè 27) stays busy until 03:00.

For gut-busting portions of vegetarian organic food, try Comme Bio (93 319 89 68, Via Laietana 28). While it's not organic (and not even strictly vegetarian), nearby Bliss Café (93 268 10 22, Plaça Sant Just 4) specialises in healthy meals, with a particularly appetising selection of salads, as well as home-made cakes. For a guaranteed sugar-rush in beautiful surroundings though, it's got to be Caelum (93 302 69 33, Carrer de la Palla 8), with its fantastic fairy cakes and pastries, to be washed down by excellent coffee.

Venue Finder

Catalan	Agut	p.166
Catalan	Andu	p.166
Catalan	Cafe de l'Academi	p.166
Catalan	Els Quatre Gats	p.167
French	Quo Vadis	p.168
Japanese	Kynoto	p.168
Mexican	Margarita Blue	p.168
Portuguese	Can Culleretes	p.167
Bar	Fonfone	p.169
Bar	Ginger	p.170
Bar	Milk	p.170
Bar	Schilling	p.170
Bar	Siddhartha	p.170
Nightclub	Club 13	p.177
Nightclub	Jamboree	p.171

Restaurants

Agut
Catalan

C/ Gignàs, 16
93 315 17 09

In a city where Catalan food is often fused with French sauces and cooking methods, this family-run restaurant offers authentic, untouched, untainted Catalan cuisine, and has remained popular for 75 years for doing so. Its historical building and 50s decor give it a retro feel, with Catalan art on every wall and a tiny bar tucked neatly into one corner.

Jaume I, Map 10 A4 **1**

Andu
Catalan

C/ Correo Viejo, 3
646 553 930

If you didn't know better, you'd think this cosy, cluttered cave of a place had been part of a Catalan family for generations; in fact, an Australian and Austrian run it. Home-cooked tapas, a decent wine list and strong drinks are the order of the day. Pull up an armchair and settle in for a long, easygoing night. Jaume I, Map 10 A3 **2**

Cafe de l'Academia
Catalan

C/ Lledo, 1
93 419 82 53

Dishes at this popular Catalan restaurant are hearty but inventive, and the tables in the little plaça outside are especially delightful. Staff speak English but the menu and decor are firmly local. Unlike many good restaurants, it also serves breakfast. The *menú del dia* is especially good value. Booking ahead is advised. Jaume I, Map 10 A3 **3**

Sangria jugs

Can Culleretes

Portuguese

C/ Quintana, 5

93 317 64 85

Established in 1786 as a pastry shop, Can Culleretes is still serving food, although these days it's more likely to be partridge than pastries. Many of the original architectural features have been preserved, making for an atmospheric setting, although this is tempered by the signed photos of film stars and matadors. Booking is essential in the summer months.  Liceu, Map 9 E2 4

Els Quatre Gats

Catalan

C/ Montsió 3 bis

93 302 41 40

Although this cafe-restaurant plays up its reputation as an early haunt of Picasso (he held his first public exhibition here) and the hangout of choice for the modernisme art circle,

Els Quatre Gats is still a worthwhile experience. The decor is flamboyantly modernisme, the menu is upmarket Catalan, and the waiters are attentive, even if prices are rather inflated.

🚇 Sant Antoni, Map 7 A3 **5**

Kynoto

Japanese

C/ de la Ciutat, 5

93 304 23 76

With its hip decor and adventurous sushi menu, it's easy to see why Kynoto is so busy at weekends. English-speaking staff are helpful and happy to give advice, the ingredients are fresh and unusual, the tunes pick up as the night progresses, and there's a great cocktail menu. During the daytime, Wi-Fi is available free. 🚇 Jaume I, Map 10 A3 **6**

Margarita Blue

Mexican

C/ Josep Anseim Clave, 6

93 412 54 89

This lively bar/restaurant specialises in lethal but tasty cocktails and delicious Mexican food with a Mediterranean twist. There are classics like fajitas and fried green tomatoes, and some daring culinary combinations. The drinks are well mixed by friendly, knowledgeable bar staff. The music is fun and danceable, and it's popular with a young, up-for-it crowd.

🚇 Drassanes, Map 11 E1 **7**

Quo Vadis

French

C/ Carme, 7

93 302 40 72

This quintessential French restaurant is a popular destination after the opera or ballet. With its deep red and blue walls, old-fashioned fanned linen napkins and charming waiters in tails

Ubiquitous Moritz

and bow ties, it's an eminently civilised place. Although there are touches of Catalan influence, the menu is dominated by classically French dishes, like frog legs, and cheese soufflé.

 Liceu, Map 7 D4 **8**

Bars

Fonfone
C/ Escudellers, 24   93 317 14 24

Orange, pink, yellow and green bubble lights illuminate the bar area, giving this small space a clubby feel. There's a tiny dancefloor with DJs every night, playing funk, electronica, house or electroclash. Around midnight, it becomes a popular stop-off point for revellers warming up for the clubs.

 Liceu, Map 9 E3 **9**

Ginger

Pl Sant Just, 1   93 310 53 09

The lights are low, the music is chilled and the seats are dangerously comfortable, so a quick pre-dinner drink has a tendency to turn into a five-hour rampage through the cocktail menu or extensive wine list. This is a relaxed spot, but it's hard not to feel cool while drinking here. Fancy tapas offers sustenance, and staff are friendly.

Jaume I, Map 10 A2 **10**

Milk

C/ Gignas, 21   93 268 09 22

Milk is chic and plush, without being intimidating or overpriced. Details like original 50s Florence Broadhurst wallpaper and hand-made sofas add a layer of decadence. The food is international, ranging from Thai curries to sausages. The 'recovery brunch' served at weekends is particularly popular among foreigners. It's one of the few bars in Barcelona with a happy hour. Jaume I, Map 10 B4 **11**

Schilling

C/ Ferran, 23   93 317 67 87

Schilling is pleasant in the day, but really comes alive at night, when it buzzes with a vibrant mix of nationalities, sexualities and ages. Good music and cocktails keep things swinging into the early hours, and excellent nibbles are available. The decor is more 20s New York than 21st century Barcelona, but that only adds to its charm.

Liceu, Map 9 E2 **12**

Siddhartha

C/ Avinyo, 26   93 301 04 22

Hermann Hesse's novel of the same name is the story of a young man's journey of self discovery. The bar in Barri Gòtic can lead you on a journey to carnage and debauchery. The combination of killer cocktails served in rather vampy candle-lit, velvet-draped surroundings can leave you with a headache as dark as the interior. 🚇 Jaume I, Map 9 F3 **13**

Nightclubs

Club 13

Pl Reial, 13   93 317 23 52

More sophisticated than the bigger *discotecas*, Club 13 combines restaurant, wine bar and nightclub. In the main area, DJs play to a dancefloor packed with a dressy crowd. This is surrounded by small, intimate seating areas, arched brickwork and a very elegant bar. 🚇 Liceu, Map 9 E3 **14**

Jamboree

Pl Reial, 17   93 319 17 89

While Jamboree had its heyday in the 60s, it's still a popular jazz and blues club. It seems like two different venues under one roof; the upstairs is a magnet for young R&B and hip-hop fans, while downstairs is a smokey jazz den that welcomes international artists. Brick archways, low lighting and wooden benches give a suitably historic feel. There's no charge before 01:00, and afterwards it'll only cost a few euros to enter.
🚇 Liceu, Map 9 D3 **15**

Born & Sant Pere

This hip, creative district is buzzing with nightlife, from the glacially cool to the laid-back and comfortable.

Great local, international and fusion restaurants crowd Born's backstreets, fighting for space with dimly-lit little cocktail bars and chilled-out cafes, where you can watch the exotically-dressed crowds do their thing. Sant Pere has a more local feel, but new places are opening rapidly.

Also In The Area

The Passeig del Born has a number of trendy spots for people-watching over a glass of wine, and many have outdoor terraces. As the name suggests, Sandwich & Friends (93 310 07 86, Passeig del Born 27) supplies bread-based sustenance; it's part of a growing local chain.

For one of the most interesting Asian places, try the relatively new Wushu (93 310 73 13, Carrer Colomines 2), which offers a small but delicious selection of dishes from Thailand, Indonesia and Japan, with ingredients coming from the spectacular Mercat de Santa Caterina (p.141) opposite. Also benefiting from market-fresh produce is the outstanding Cuines Santa Caterina (93 268 99 18, Avinguda Francesc Cambó 20), a sleek space with great cooking.

For a taste of a different part of Spain, head to Basque bar Euskal Etxea (93 310 21 85, Placeta Montcada 1-3), which serves pinxos – bread topped with foul-sounding but delicious tasting combinations of anchovies, peppers, meats and pastes. Load up your plate and keep the cocktail sticks, which will be used to calculate your bill.

Tucked away but still madly popular is the 30s style champagne bar El Xampanyet (93 319 70 03, Carrer Montcada 22), an antique-strewn little place on the gothic streets near the Picasso Museum. Home to cheap drinks, good tapas and a lively crowd made up of ageing locals and young foreigners.

Quieter, leafy Sant Pere has a constantly-changing roster of quirky little bars; Sant Pere Mes Alt has a particularly good string of them.

Venue Finder

Restaurants

Abac
C/ Rec, 79-89

Fusion
93 319 66 00

This French-Spanish cuisine has wowed royalty and while it's not expensive, you do have to book. For the effort, you get unobtrusively attentive service, exquisite decor and superb food. Suckling pig is a house speciality. 🚇 Jaume I, Map 10 D3 **16**

Arrel del Born
C/ Fusina, 5

Seafood
93 319 92 99

Chef Manuel Diaz is known for his seafood. Heavily influenced by Catalan flavours, he creates simple dishes like sautéed langoustine with onions. The menu and ingredients change every season, so he's permanently working on new creations, drawing back loyal crowds. 🚇 Arc de Triomf, Map 10 E3 **17**

Bossborn Tapes
Pl de Palau, 13

Spanish
93 295 58 66

This looks like a classic tapas spot, but has a youthful atmosphere, largely thanks to the boundless energy of its young owner, Albert Bosser. A delightful little place that blends fresh tapas ideas, like bull meat, with well-executed classics like tortilla and patatas bravas. 🚇 Barceloneta, Map 10 C4 **18**

Cal Pep
Pl de les Olles, 8

Seafood
93 310 79 61

This tapas bar is famous for its seafood, and for Pep himself, who is usually hovering behind the long bar, smiling brightly and greeting everyone. Choose your fish and watch it cooked in front of you, or opt for one of the many meat dishes, such as beef stew. 🚇 Barceloneta, Map 10 D4 **19**

Comerç 24
C/ Comerç, 24

Spanish
93 319 21 02

Carles Abellan's restaurant serves up adventurous modern Spanish cuisine, which verges on being overly stylised (eggshells filled with egg foam), but Comerç 24 is a serious foodie destination. Prices are high, and the atmosphere is intimate. 🚇 Arc de Triomf, Map 10 E1 **20**

El Pebre Blau
C/ Banys Vells, 21

Moroccan
93 319 13 08

El Pebre Blau is one of the few places that successfully blends Moroccan and Catalan cuisine, and even some Indian twists. Restaurant space is small but not cramped, and arches add to the intimacy. Chef Teresa Ferri provides lots of sweet and savoury combinations, and a great selection of salads.
🚇 Jaume I, Map 10 C3 **21**

Taller de Tapas
Pl Sant Josep

Spanish
93 268 85 59

Part of a growing chain, Taller de Tapas has hit on a great mix, providing fair-priced traditional and modern tapas using fantastically fresh ingredients. The wine list isn't enormous, but it's very carefully chosen. Booking ahead is recommended, especially for an outside table. 🚇 Liceu, Map 9 E2 **22**

Bars

Barroc Cafe

C/ Rec, 67   93 268 46 23

A cafe by day, at night one hip little spot. As the name suggests, there's a Baroque splendour to this place: faux candelabras adorn the ceiling, and gilt and red velvet dominate. In-house DJs spin lounge tunes to a good-looking gay and straight crowd. 🚇 Tetuan, Map 4 E4 23

Café de la Ribera

Pl de les Olles, 6   93 319 50 72

Smack in the centre of Born, Cafe de la Ribera is a throwback to the Barcelona of the 30s. This is a good spot for a daytime drink, but is especially lovely at night with its cosy spaces lined with Spanish tiles, wood panelling and beautiful Parisian-style chairs. 🚇 Barceloneta, Map 10 D4 24

Crepes del Born

Pg del Born, 12   93 269 03 25

This little establishment concentrates on cocktails and crepes in the middle of the very hip Passeig del Born. It's a great spot for people-watching, with jugglers, bongo drummers and hipsters strutting about outside. 🚇 Jaume I, Map 10 C4 26

El Monasterio

Pg d'Isabel II   www.salamonasterio.com

In this warren of drinking holes, it is easy to forget you are just a stone's throw from the lapping tide. The cafe serves snacks and tapas from early morning until the wee small hours, while the main bar draws in late-night revellers. There is an eclectic programme, with frequent live jazz and film screenings ensuring that it is a regular haunt for arty types.

🚇 Barceloneta, Map 12 B1 **25**

Gimlet
C/ Rec, 24

This tiny, yet legendary bar is always packed with a friendly crowd with one thing in common: the protracted enjoyment of some of the best cocktails in town. There's nothing fussy about Gimlet: no offers or happy hours, just a tried-and-tested combination of elegant retro decor and expert barmen.

🚇 Jaume I, Map 10 D3 **27**

La Vinya del Senyor
Pl Santa Maria, 5   93 310 33 79

This is a charming location to spend an evening, and has an extensive wine and cava list. Facing the spectacular Santa Maria Church (p.71), there's a small but delectable tapas menu and if you're lucky enough to get the tiny top room, you'll benefit from some great views.

🚇 Jaume I, Map 10 C2 **28**

Princesa 23
C/ Princesa, 23   93 268 86 19

Princesa 23 serves up tapas and sandwiches all day, giving it a cafe feel until about 22:00, when it becomes a lively bar with chilled-out music and an amiable crowd. There are plenty of

Moroccan-style loungers and scatter cushions to recline on, and the TV shows live sport.

Rubí

C/ dels Banys Vells 6 bis   93 310 68 24

This 'supper club' seamlessly bridges the bar-restaurant divide. Kicking off earlier than most restaurants, it morphs into a bar as the night progresses, with funky, upbeat tunes and a good selection of wines and cocktails. The blood-red walls and candlelit tables add to the intimacy of this seductive little place. ⬛ Jaume I, Map 10 C3 29

Salero

C/ Rec, 60   93 319 80 22

Although part of Salero is a restaurant, it's best for cocktails. Whitewashed walls, white lilies, candlelight and Moroccan furniture create a wonderful atmosphere, and tapas and sushi are available until late. A great place to stop off after supper or for a pre-dinner mojito. ⬛ Jaume I, Map 10 D3 30

Nightclubs

Club Mix

C/ Comerç 21   93 319 46 96

This tiny club, which opened in early 2007, has a retro disco feel, with chocolate leather seating and glitter balls. It's a fun, intimate little place, with crowd-pleasing funk and soul classics and strong drinks. Popular with foreigners, as well as Born-dwelling trendies. ⬛ Jaume I, Map 10 E2 31

Club Mix

Barceloneta & The Beaches

Head to the water's edge for all the seafood you can handle, whether in a fancy restaurant or pavement bar.

Between Barceloneta and Vila Olímpica, the waterfront has an almost continuous string of restaurants, most of which (predictably) specialise in fish. A couple of streets back from Barceloneta's main drag is a great collection of lively, local tapas bars, while out towards the towers of Hotel Arts and Torre Mapfre are some swisher destinations.

Also In The Area

There are more bars and restaurants in this district than could possibly be visited, but as you'd expect from such a touristy zone they can tend towards the generic; the ones along Passeig Joan de Borbó and around the Port Olímpic can be especially samey. A street away from Joan de Borbó, Salamanca (93 221 50 33, Carrer Almirall Cervera 34 & 27) stands out for having such an enormous terrace – this is one place where it's hard not to get a good seat.

For something a little more upmarket, head to one of the restaurants on the ground floor of the Palau del Mar, such as Merendero de la Mari (93 221 31 41, Plaça Pau Vila 1), where slick service and imaginative entrées and desserts frame an excellent selection of seafood. There are also great views of Port Vell. For a drink and a nibble in the marina rather than next to it, try Luz de Gas (93 484 23 26, moored in front of Palau del Mar), which is housed in a rather sleek yacht. It's a quietly romantic little spot. For a big night out, Port Olímpic offers a fair selection of bars. The music is straight from the charts and the crowd is largely young and foreign, but it's lively most nights – even during the week when many places in town are quieter.

Venue Finder

Restaurants

7 Portes   Portuguese
Pg d'Isabel II, 14   93 319 30 33

Located in Barcelonaeta, this is one of the oldest restaurants in the city, having served seafood since 1836. With non-stop service from lunch until supper, it's usually buzzing, attracting both tourists and loyal locals. Fish dishes are skinned and deboned at the table.

 Barceloneta, Map 12 C1 **32**

Arola
Spanish

C/ Marina, 19-21, Hotel Arts
93 483 80 90

This hip spot, run by Michelin-starred chef Sergi Arola, faces the sea from inside the Hotel Arts. There's an airy dining room, fab menu, attentive but unobtrusive service, and a terrace with sofas. Come for DJs, cocktails and gourmet nibbles with a sea view. 🚇 Ciutadella/Vila Olímpica, Map 14 B2 **33**

Agua
Mediterranean

Pg Marítim de la Barceloneta, 30
93 225 12 72

Agua, near the Hotel Arts, has a wide terrace that slopes right onto the ocean, as well as a dining room with great views and high windows. Seafood and fish are the stars of the show; huge display cases show off the catches of the day, which are then grilled over an open fire.

🚇 Ciutadella/Vila Olímpica, Map 14 A3 **34**

Els Pescadors
Seafood

Pl Prim, 1
93 225 20 18

Old-fashioned and deeply charming, this is one of the city's best fish restaurants and well worth the journey, if only for its bacallà (salted cod). A gorgeous terrace looks across a tranquil plaça, and much of the interior has been carefully preserved.

🚇 Poblenou, Map 1 E3

Kaiku
Mediterranean

Pl del Mar, 1
93 221 90 82

Plenty of Barcelona eateries serve paella, but Kaiku takes the experience to another level: try smoked rice (an unappetising grey-green colour, but absolutely delicious) or black rice (made with squid ink). 🚇 Barceloneta, Map 12 D3 38

Bars

Bestial
C/ Ramon Trias Fargas, 2-4   93 224 04 07
Although it offers a huge array of Italian-Catalan fusion food, Bestial is best as a bar. Its waterfront terrace and chic interior manage to be warm but sleek, airy and minimalist. A popular destination for fashion and media types, it can get packed at the weekends, but somehow it remains extremely relaxed.

🚇 Ciutadella/Vila Olímpica, Map 14 B2 35

Fritz Mar
Pg Maritim de Barceloneta, 34   93 221 77 65
This beach bar on the edge of the sand has an Italian kitchen and great music, but its real selling point is its terrace, with comfortable seating and water views, it also catches a cool breeze from the Med. It's busy year-round, attracting the young and trendy revellers of Barceloneta.

🚇 Ciutadella/Vila Olímpica, Map 14 A3 36

Jai-Ca
C/ Ginebra 13   93 319 50 02
Jai-Ca is a traditional tapas bar where the order of the day is great seafood at rock-bottom prices. It can get extremely noisy and crowded, but it's fun; tell the waiter you're there

and sip a beer on the pavement while you wait for a table on the miniscule terrace. 🍴 Barceloneta, Map 12 D3 **37**

Nightclubs

Baja Beach Club

Pg Marítim de Barceloneta, 34   93 225 91 00

Officially the largest dance space in Barcelona, this is very much a club, despite the presence of a large restaurant. Decorated in kitsch 80s Miami Beach style, Baja's real draw is its very late opening hours, and live DJs spinning plenty of salsa, samba and Brazilian music. 🍴 Ciutadella/Vila Olímpica, Map 14 A2 **39**

Carpe Diem

Pg Marítim de Barceloneta, 32   93 224 04 70

Excellent DJs, luxurious interiors and highly-trained mixologists make Carpe Diem worth a visit. Before midnight it's a lovely place to wine and dine, while after midnight things pick up and keep pumping until dawn. 🍴 Ciutadella/Vila Olímpica, Map 14 A2 **40**

Catwalk

C/ Ramon Trias Fargas, 24   93 221 61 61

When DJs fly from as far away as New York to play a venue, it should be a winner. This is a clubber's paradise, but not as intense as some other venues. There are two dancefloors, one dedicated to dance tunes, and another with R&B and hip-hop. White canopy couches provide chill-out space. Catwalk boasts Miami glitz without the pretention.

🍴 Ciutadella/Vila Olímpica, Map 14 B1 **41**

Arty restaurant interiors

Raval

For cheap eats and a lively, alternative vibe, Raval is a great destination, with new venues regularly opening.

Less obviously touristy than the Barri Gòtic and less trend-conscious than Born, Raval's nightlife is packed with people just looking for a good time. Traditionally an impoverished part of town, Raval still has plenty of affordable eateries with a particularly dense concentration of curry houses and fusion places. The seedy element remains, with some fairly verbal prostitutes between carrers Sant Pau and l'Hospital, but this is a good area for a drink. The bars come in two basic types: ancient but venerable dens of iniquity, and newly opened, swish cocktail joints.

Also In The Area

There's some lovely, relaxed drinking and dining to be done in and around the MACBA/CCCB compound: try one of the cafes facing onto the plaça for a leisurely, tasty lunch or an afternoon beer. Plaça dels Àngels (93 329 40 47, Carrer Ferlandina 23) is the closest to the skaters and trendy kids of the plaça. The lunch deal is particularly good value. Inside the gallery compound itself, CE Bar (93 301 33 15, Carrer Montalegre 5), is another good lounging spot, serving lunch and supper; at night, DJs and live acts pick up the pace a little.

At the bottom of Rambla de Raval, a clutch of kooky, cosy little bars provide great chilled-out surroundings in the daytime and a buzzy, lively atmosphere at night. There's Ambar (no phone, Carrer Sant Pau 77), and Madame Jasmine (607 88 04 43, Rambla de Raval 22). Pull up a junkshop chair in a corner of either of these fun little haunts for coffee, herbal tea and snacks in the daytime, or squeeze in for cocktails and spirits at night.

For bar-hopping, try Carrer Joaquín Costa, where fun, eclectic little bars like Benidorm (no phone, Carrer Joaquín Costa 39) stand by more sophisticated watering holes such as Lletraferit (93 301 19 61, Carrer Joaquín Costa 43). The latter although bustling at night, is an enjoyable cafe during the day, offering cocktails and chilled tunes, along with a selection of books in most major European languages. A great place to sit and wait for somebody.

Venue Finder

Restaurants

Carmelitas
Doctor Dou, 1

Catalan

93 412 46 84

The restaurant focuses on Catalan dishes, made with market-fresh ingredients from the nearby Boqueria. In a nod to modern tastes, there are decent enough veggie and health-conscious options, while the wine list is a whistle-stop tour of Catalonia's tastiest and most respected vinyards.

🚇 Catalunya, Map 7 C3 49

Ca l'Isidre
C/ Flors, 12

Fusion

93 441 11 39

Family-run Ca l'Isidre is part of Raval's history: delicacies like baby octopus and lamb in truffle sauce have been drawing pop stars and art students alike for decades. The wine list is huge and Isidre himself will gladly give you some friendly advice, while his daughter, a master pastry chef, provides an outstanding array of desserts.

🚇 Paral·lel, Map 6 F3 42

Mastroque
C/ Còdols, 29

French

93 301 79 42

This trendy bar and restaurant serves up a menu of elegantly simple Provençal cookery with a few Catalan dishes thrown in, all washed down with a decent selection of French, Catalan and Spanish wines. The ambience is sleek and stylish, and it's a great place to go, whether for a couple of drinks or a full meal. 🚇 Drassanes, Map 11 E1 43

Bars

Aurora

C/ Aurora, 7   93 422 30 44

Deep red walls provide a striking backdrop to electronic beats here. Open until dawn at weekends, this is where you can expect lots of mohawks, mullets, dreadlocks, and a very friendly, alternative atmosphere. 🚇 Sant Antoni, Map 9 A1 **44**

Bar Lobo

C/ Pintor Fortuny, 3   93 442 72 63

This cavernous, black-and-white bar is very cool, but remains welcoming. Behind a huge bar, attractive staff serve an impressive selection of drinks. There's outdoor seating and a small but appetising menu. 🚇 Catalunya, Map 7 E3 **45**

Bar Marsella

C/ Sant Pau, 65   93 481 53 46

Many Spanish bars claim to have hosted Hemingway, who was known to like a drink. Bar Marsella, however, served Picasso, Miró and Gaudí too. You get an absinthe sugar cube with each drink, to encourage creativity. 🚇 Liceu, Map 9 B2 **46**

Bar Pastis

C/ Santa Monica, 4   93 318 79 80

A love of Edith Piaf and Paris inspired Carme Pericas and Quime Ballester to open Bar Pastis, back in the 40s. Piaf's music still plays long into the night, attracting a bohemian crowd to this charmingly chaotic little bar. 🚇 Drassanes, Map 11 D1 **47**

Boadas

C/ Tallers, 1   93 318 95 92

Cuban Miguel Boadas opened his wood-panelled little
cocktail bar in the 40s, and it's now run by his daughter,
Maria Dolores. The cocktail list has a number of drinks
designed by Miguel himself, which are named after local
landmarks. A relaxed spot for a quality drink.

🔲 Catalunya, Map 7 E2 **48**

Kasparo

Pl Vicens Martorell, 4   93 302 20 72

This bar-cafe is in a very peaceful little square, shielded from
much of the hectic bustle of Raval. Alongside alcoholic and
non-alcoholic drinks, it boasts a tempting and varied menu
that offers both tapas and Thai curry. The two Australian
owners never close the kitchen.

🔲 Catalunya, Map 7 D2 **50**

Sant Pau 68

C/ Sant Pau, 68

Another Raval venue that metamorphoses from a daytime
restaurant into a late-night bar. At midnight, Sant Pau's
restaurant settings are cleared away in record time and
opened out into a dance floor. Popular among those turned
off by swanky, pretentious bars, it focuses on good music
and strong cocktails, while ensuring everyone has enough
room to dance. 🔲 Liceu, Map 7 B2 **51**

Silenus

C/ Angels, 8   93 302 26 80

Another hybrid Barcelona venue, Silenus advertises itself
as a restaurant but is delightful as a cafe and bar during
the day and early evening. There are beautiful stained
glass doors and chunky old wooden tables to sit at, while
knowledgeable staff can recommend the best bottle from
an extensive wine list. 🚇 Catalunya, Map 7 C3 52

Nightclubs

Club Apolo

C/ Nou de la Rambla, 113   93 301 00 90

Club Apolo is a converted ballroom that hosts live concerts,
shows and visual events through the week, and transforms
into Nitsaclub at weekends. A marathon of techno,
electronica and house attracts a young and dedicated clan of
dancers. The serious crowds (and queues) start at 04:00.
🚇 Paral·lel, Map 6 F4 53

Moog

C/ Arc del Teatre, 3   93 301 49 91

While the 05:00 finish is unfashionably early here, tiny
Moog still has a loyal following. Open every night, it is
staunchly committed to high-quality techno and house, with
international guest DJs most Wednesday nights, and plenty of
local talent the rest of the week. 🚇 Liceu, Map 9 C4 54

Montjuïc & Poble Sec

Head to the hill for fine dining with spectacular city views, or discover Poble Sec's quirky, charismatic bars.

The city-facing slope of Montjuïc is peppered with some excellent restaurants. There are also some fine, secluded bars, where you can enjoy knockout city views. The streets around Plaça d'Espanya are home to a range of excellent bars and huge clubs, while Poble Sec's handful of restaurants are some of Barcelona's best-kept secrets.

Also In The Area

One of the city's most chilled-out spots has to be La Caseta de Migdia (no phone; www.lacaseta.org, Passeig del Migdia s/n), near to the castle at Montjuïc's summit. It's an intimate, candle-lit opening in the forest, scattered with deck chairs and tables and soothing tunes, to help contemplate the cityscape below. At busy times there's often a barbecue, too. It's best enjoyed on warm summer nights.

Further down the hill, Poble Espanyol (p.87) hosts the open-air club Terrrazza (93 272 49 80, Avinguda Marques de Comillas s/n, www.laterrrazza.com) at weekends in the summer. The pretty little square of the tourist village is an unlikely setting for the superstar DJs and frenetic crowds, but it works, leading to some very late nights.

Among the other clubs in the area is the recently opened Sala Instinto (no phone, Carrer Méjico 7), a two-room place with some alternative nights of reggae, downbeat and hip-hop providing a little respite from the city's almost universal thumping house and techno.

Meanwhile, down in Poble Sec, little bars like Sólo Bar (93 338 76 18, Carrer Margarit 18) demonstrate why the district is so worth exploring. A quirky little place beloved by locals, Sólo is easygoing but lively, with live bands in the evenings, and affordable beers and tapas to be enjoyed while browsing the multilingual books and comics.

Venue Finder

Italian	La Bella Napoli	p.193
Mediterranean	Montjuïc El Xalet	p.194
Bar	Salsitas	p.194
Gay & Lesbian	Gay Day at Space	p.195
Gay & Lesbian	Quimet i Quimet	p.194

Restaurants

La Bella Napoli
C/ Margarit, 14

Italian

93 442 50 56

The Neapolitan owners of La Bella Napoli certainly contribute to the authenticity of this fantastic Italian. Excitable, noisy and prone to *Godfather*-style hand gestures, they add a layer of buzz and excitement to the popular, traditionally decorated dining room. Naturally, pizza and pasta dishes are perennial favourites, and can be ordered to eat in or takeway, but it's worth exploring the more adventurous Italian classics. Save room for the tiramisu.

🚇 Paral·lel, Map 6 E3 73

Montjuïc El Xalet

Mediterranean

Av Miramar, 31

93 324 92 70

In a crisp building with jaw-dropping views across the city lies this gem of a restaurant, serving Mediterranean cuisine that's creative and daring without being just plain silly. It's a moderately pricey option, but expect unusual ingredients used skilfully in a winning combination of texture and flavour. It's good for very elegant lunching between gallery visits.

Map 1 B4

Quimet i Quimet

Spanish

C/Poeta Cabanyes, 25

25 934 42 31 42

One of the city's most beloved tapas bars, everything about Quimet i Quimet is classic, from the haughty waiters to the cramped quarters. Still, it's worth the squeeze for the food; it specialises in gourmet preserved seafoods (which are a lot tastier than they sound) and montaditos (bread topped with delicious combinations of ingredients). 🚇 Poble Sec, Map 6 E3 **75**

Bars

Salsitas

C/ Nou de la Rambla, 22

93 318 08 40

The fresh tropical fruit cocktails served at Salsitas are matched by the cheesiness of the decor, but don't let that put you off. The bar here is massive and there is a beautiful, all-white dining room. It draws a glamorous young crowd due to the excellent music and large dancefloor; there's also a chill-out area with comfortable sofas. 🚇 Liceu, Map 9 C3 **74**

Plaça d'Espanya

Gay & Lesbian

Gay Day at Space
C/ Tarragona, 141   93 467 59 71

A franchise of the world-famous Space Ibiza, Space in Barcelona is most famous for its men-only gay day, every Sunday. Expect a hedonistic, uninhibited atmosphere, top music and spectacular dance shows. Other nights are mixed but still immensely popular among the local gay community.

Tarragona, Map 3 B3 76

Eixample

With Michelin-starred restaurants and smokey tapas bars, there's plenty going on after dark in swanky Eixample.

In the daytime, Eixample has a solidly residential feel, with cafes and restaurants scattered through its broad, straight streets. But parts of the district come alive at night and it's particularly good for classy international dining and gay venues.

Also In The Area

This is a great area for carnivores, with plenty of Latin American places serving juicy steaks fresh off the flames. Try El Boliche del Gordo Cabrera (93 215 68 81, Carrer Consell de Cent, 338) or Patagonia (93 304 37 35, Gran Via Corts Catalanes, 660). For Argentinean flavour, Pampero (93 532 17 51, Plaça Doctor Letamendi, 25) has live tango bands on Tuesday evenings.

Vegetarian options are a tad less glamorous: the cafe Amaltea (93 454 86 13, Carrer Diputació 164) specialises in oversized portions of meat-free dishes. Two chains that are good for a meat-free vitamin hit are Fresc & Co (93 301 68 37, Carrer Pau Claris, 51) and Fresh & Ready (93 216 03 39, Passeig de Gràcia, 46), which sells particularly good fruit juices. Further up the scale is Habaluc (93 452 29 28, Carrer Enric Granados, 41), which specialises in creative vegetarian food, but also has a couple of meat dishes.

Al Jaima (93 454 07 12, Carrer València, 218) serves up good Arabic food and sheesha pipes. Baravins (93 451 51

72, Carrer Comte D'urgell, 196) is authentically French, complete with snails and roquefort fondue. Cata 181 (93 323 68 18, Carrer Valencia, 181) is a fantastic example of modern Spanish cuisine. Il Commendatore (93 322 55 53, Carrer Comte D'Urgell, 247) does great Italian, and Noti (93 342 66 73, Carrer Roger de Lluria, 35-37) serves good Mediterranean food to beautiful people while enticing Jazz music plays in the background. Eixample is also home to the notorious 'Gaixample', centred on the junction of Carrers Aribau and Diputació. This is a cluster of raucous gay bars and clubs, including Arena (93 487 83 42, Carrer Balmes 32, www.arenadisco.com) and Metro (93 323 52 27, C/Sepúlveda, 185).

Venue Finder

Restaurants

Can Gaig
C/ d'Arago, 214

Catalan
93 429 10 17

Can Gaig is a local family favourite. The signature dish is roast partridge with Iberian bacon, and there's a good wine and cigar selection. It has been family-owned for generations and has a welcoming atmosphere. 🚇 Universitat, Map 4 B3 55

El Rodizio
Av Diagonal, 477

Brazilian
93 319 17 89

Great for budget dining, this fixed-price buffet serves some of Barcelona's best Brazilian food (and devilishly strong cocktails). The buffet is vast, and well-cooked meat is served directly to your table. Skip lunch if you're planning supper here: you'll need all the belly-space you can get. 🚇 Girona, Map 4 F3 56

Gorria
C/ Diputacio, 421

Basque
93 245 11 64

All the ingredients at this family-run restaurant hail from Navarra and the Basque country, as do many of the cooking methods. The desserts are exceptional, and a huge wine cellar holds regional Spanish favourites. There's a waiting list for a table, but it's well worth the effort. 🚇 Monumental, Map 5 B4 57

Jaume de Provença
C/ Provença, 88

French
93 430 00 29

Rumoured to be a favourite of King Juan Carlos, this excellent, rustic-style French restaurant (with a slight Catalan twist) has won three major European awards for its modern menu. Signature dishes include sole stuffed with mushrooms, and rabbit loins. 🚇 Entença, Map 3 D1 **58**

La Bodegueta

Spanish

Rla de Catalunya, 100

93 215 48 66

You'd find it hard to find better tapas than the selection served up here. The decor is old-fashioned, the atmosphere is smokey, it's always busy, and the waiters are grumpy. But, La Bodegueta will bring you back time and again, for perfect pimientos de padron, mouthwatering steak tartare and tongue-tingling anchovies. 🚇 Diagonal, Map 4 C2 **59**

La Dama

Catalan

Av Diagonal, 423

93 202 06 86

Set on the first floor of a stunning art nouveau building, this Michelin-starred restaurant specialises in modern Catalan cuisine. Knowledgeable waiters are happy to advise on the excellent wine list. Reservations are required and the dress code is smart. 🚇 Diagonal, Map 8 B4 **60**

Tragaluz

Mediterranean

Ptge de la Concepció, 5

93 487 01 96

Tragaluz has a strong reputation, enhanced by its menu of Mediterranean classics and novel, sliding roof. There are three floors, with the Mezzanine lounge usually the most popular, while more casual Tragarapid is downstairs, and across the street is the Japanese version.

🚇 Provença, Map 4 C1 **61**

Bars

Buda Bar

C/ Pau Claris, 92   93 318 95 92

Buda is glam and opulent. The gothic-oriental interior surrounds
scantily-clad staff serving exotic cocktails. The atmosphere is
buzzing, the music loud and unless you get there unfashionably
early, you'll need to book ahead. 🚇 Passeig de Gràcia, Map 2 E2 **62**

Public

C/ Rossello, 277

With its purple-hued backdrop, artwork (all for sale) and
outside seating, Public is a great, trendy pit stop. This is a
quiet, relaxed cafe by day, that transforms into a heaving bar
at night, with an arty clientele. 🚇 Diagonal, Map 4 D1 **63**

Nightclubs

Club Zac

Av Diagonal, 477   93 319 17 89

Club Zac offers a welcome respite from dance and techno
music. With a fun, danceable menu of funk, soul, jazz,
Motown and flamenco, there are live shows until 02:00, after
which the all-night clubbing begins. 🚇 Fontana, Map1 B2

Omm Session

C/ Rosselló, 265   93 445 40 00

Attached to the groovy new Hotel Omm, this is a good spot
for a post-dinner cocktail, or for some all-night dancing. The

sleek furnishings, infectious tunes and well-crafted drinks
make it very popular. 🚇 Diagonal, Map 4 D1 **64**

Gay & Lesbian

Café Miranda
C/ Pau Claris, 92   93 318 95 92

This gay cabaret restaurant and bar draws huge crowds, and
provides unashamed fun. The restaurant is excellent and with
separate bar and lounge areas it is good for cocktails too.
Drag queens entertain with live shows, music is sensationally
kitsch and the interior is like a Hans Christian Andersen tale.
🚇 Universitat, Map 4 A4 **65**

Sweet Café
C/ Casanova, 75   www.sweetcafebcn.blogspot.com

There isn't much cafe-like about this new player on the gay
scene. Open until 03:00, it's a pre-clubbing venue for those
who want cocktails and good music. The crowd is mostly gay,
but everyone is welcome. It also hosts short film festivals and
other cultural events. 🚇 Urgell, Map 4 A3 **66**

Z:eltas
C/ Casanova, 75   93 451 84 69

This excellent cocktail bar is open to all but draws a largely
gay crowd. With its glowing orange interiors and strong
cocktails, it's relaxed early in the evening, but later on, drags
and gorgeous waiters often get on the bar to start the
dancing. 🚇 Urgell, Map 4 A3 **66**

Above Eixample

With lively, bohemian Gràcia and well-heeled, elegant Sarrià, there's plenty to make a trip up the hill worthwhile.

The wealthy folk of Sarrià and Sant Gervasi regard themselves as slightly distant from downtown Barcelona, and so have exclusive, groomed bars and restaurants on the hillside. Gràcia, meanwhile, has a flair all of its own, which can be savoured in the small streets and squares.

Also In The Area

Not far from Sarrià, Les Corts also has a little cluster of sleek cocktail joints, clubs and smart restaurants. Try elegant dining and adventurous Mediterranean cuisine with a twist at Negro (93 405 94 44, Avignuda Diagonal, 640). Rub shoulders with the beautiful people in opulent, circus-themed surroundings at Elephant (93 334 02 58, Passeig dels Til·lers, 1) or dance the night away at the Barcelona branch of Balearic super-club Pachá (93 334 33 23, Avignuda Doctor Marañón, 17). During the weekends in the summer months, there's also the Ibiza-styled La Sal (no telephone, Avinguda Manuel Azaña 21-23). Gràcia is also well worth exploring. Its lively streets and squares contain many bars and restaurants, including some great international options. It's home to Barcelona's only Iraqi restaurant, Mesopotamia (93 237 15 63, Carrer Verdi 65) and its only Ethiopian, Abissínia (93 213 07 85, Carrer Torrent de les Flors 55). For decent, MSG free Chinese, there's the very friendly Memorias de China (93 415 76 02, Carrer Lincoln, 17), and excellent Moroccan, Turkish and Lebanese options. Meanwhile, there's ample bar-hopping: start with a drink and a snack on a terrace in Plaça del Sol (Map 2) before enjoying cocktails and local DJs at Mond Bar (no telephone, Plaça del Sol, 21).

Venue Finder

Restaurants

Botafumeiro
Seafood

C/ El Gran de Gràcia, 81   93 218 42 30

A firm favourite locally, Botafumeiro's fantastic Galician seafood has also been enjoyed by Bill Clinton and Woody Allen. The decor is classic: think wooden walls, crisp fresh linen and a gallery of floodlit tables. A huge range of Galician white wine is available to accompany the food. Tapas and raciones can be eaten at the bar. 🚇 Fontana, Map 2 D3 57

Brilliant Lounge
Mediterranean

C/ Balmes, 314   93 414 58 04

A prime destination for dinner and dancing rolled into one, Brilliant Lounge offers fresh Mediterranean food, great cocktails and live DJs. It's a hip, bustling joint that works hard to stay fresh, with up-to-the-minute decor, music and dishes: expect ostrich fillet steak and other exotic delicacies. The dining room and bar are separate, so it's not too noisy.

Lesseps, Map 1 C1

Can Punyetes
Catalan

C/ Maria Cubi, 189   93 200 91 59

Although it's part of a Spain-wide franchise, nothing about Can Punyetes feels corporate: instead, the atmosphere is quaint and family-run. The decor is slightly shambolic and strewn with antiques, and there's an unpretentious, rustic charm and warmth. Affordable but quality pates, cheeses, meats and anchovies pile out the kitchen by the platter-load, day and night. Lesseps, Map 1 B1

El Racó d'en Freixa
Catalan

C/ Sant Elies, 22   93 209 75 59

Run by the Freixa family for years, this restaurant garnered a whole new level of buzz when son Ramon took over. Now a Spanish celebrity chef, published author and television star, Ramon has really put Catalan on the culinary map with his daring interpretations of classic dishes, with some new innovative choices such as fennel icecream.

Lesseps, Map 2 B1 68

Jean Luc Figueras

Fusion

C/ Sant Teresa, 10
93 415 28 77

In a city where food trends regularly change, Figueras works hard to maintain his place as one of Barcelona's top chefs. The seafood and meat dishes on the menu are quite traditional, but bear Figueras' telltale innovative touches. This is special occasion dining and a great excuse to head into Gràcia for supper. The service is impeccable.

Diagonal, Map 2 D4 **69**

La Rosa del Desierto

Moroccan

Pl Narcis Oller, 7
93 237 45 90

Barcelona's oldest Moroccan restaurant, La Rosa del Desierto is special. With its vast range of tagines, 10 types of couscous, kemia (an assortment of tapas) and home-made Arabic pastries for dessert, it's spawned a crowd of imitators. Still, in this case the original really is the best, and its tent-like decor and occasional belly dancing shows keep clients loyal.

Diagonal, Map 2 C4 **70**

Bars

Esbaskah

C/ Riera de Sant Miguell, 55
www.esbaskah.com

Although it's absolutely tiny, Eskasbah has a big personality and a loyal following. The focus is on music, with quality house, techno and old school classics remixed nightly by some seriously talented Catalan DJs. Dancing is what Esbaskah is all about. Fontana, Map 2 C3 **80**

Just In Bar

C/ Tusset, 28   93 415 70 32

Grinding bodies on the dance floor, pumping tunes and flowing cocktails are the general vibe here after 23:00 every night. Before that, this is quite a relaxed and tranquil place for a drink. 🚇 Gràcia, Map 2 B3 🚈

Mirablau

Final Av Tibidabo   93 418 58 79

Half-way up Tibidabo mountain, this bar boasts fantastic views. At night it's particularly stunning, as Barcelona is a blaze of lights below the large windows. Prices are a little inflated and the music is commercial, but the views more than make up for this. Map 1 C1

Up & Down

C/ Numancia, 179   93 205 51 94

Split onto two levels, upstairs usually attracts the dapper, post-theatre crowd, while the dancefloor downstairs draws younger revellers. Scruffy dressers sometimes get turned away, and there's a cover charge, although if you eat in the restaurant this is waived. 🚇 Maria Cristina, Map 1 B1

Nightclubs

Otto Zutz

C/ Lincoln, 15   93 238 07 22

Boasting eight different bars over three floors, Otto Zutz is hugely popular, satisfying a range of tastes. There's a floor

Omm Session

for loud, heavy house; another for funk and hip hop, and another for soul. There are regular organised parties and live jazz concerts (these almost always sell out), but any night guarantees great tunes and cocktails.

Fontana, Map 2 C2 **72**

Partycular

Av Tibidabo, 61   93 211 62 61

This club, which enforces a dress code, is hidden behind an unmarked doorway on the way to Tibidabo mountain. Behind that door is one of the secrets of Barcelona's elite: a welcoming place that serves killer cocktails with good music and breathtaking views across the city. The old mansion has a large dancefloor, surrounded by intimate little corners. Map 1 C1

Entertainment

Barcelona's cultural scene is throbbing with events, boasting a packed calendar of cultural festivals, gigs and shows.

Comedy

For a city where the official languages are Spanish and Catalan, there's a surprising amount of English-language stand-up. There are two monthly nights, the Giggling Guiri (Café-Teatre Llantiol, Carrer Riereta 7, www.comedyinspain. com), and the Guinness Laughter Lounge (La Riereta Teatre, Carrer Reina Amalia 3, www.gloungebcn.com), both of which ship in a highly respectable roster of promising British, American, Irish and Australian acts, often straight from the Edinburgh Festival.

For stand-up the noisy way, head to Anti-Karaoke each Wednesday night at Sidecar (Plaça Reial 7, www.antikaraoke. com). Although everybody gets a turn to belt out Guns 'n' Roses or George Michael on the mic, the star of the show is the fast-thinking and hilarious MC Rachel Arieff, who punctuates the show with a running commentary in both English and Spanish.

Live Music

This is a musical town. The Catalan love of *festas* brings music into the streets at any opportunity, and Barcelona's immigrant communities from Cuba and central and south America, add a flavour to street parties that can be distinctly un-European.

Music Venues

Apolo			
C/ Nou de la Rambla 113	93 441 40 01	www.sala-apolo.com	
Bikini			
C/ Deu i Mata 105,	93 322 08 00	www.bikinibcn.com	
Harlem Jazz Club			
C/ Comtessa de Sobradiel	89 331 00 755	na	
La Cova del Drac			
C/ Vallmajor	93 200 70 32	na	
Luz de Gas			
C/ Muntaner 246,	93 414 16 99	www.luzdegas.com	
Razzmatazz			
C/ Pamplona	93 272 09 10	www.salarazzmatazz.com	
Sidecar Factory			
Club Pl Reial	93 302 15 86	www.sidecarfactoryclub.com	

It is a firm fixture on the European tour circuit, and stadium gigs are generally held in the Palau Sant Jordi (p.86), but plenty of big acts play at venues such as Razzmatazz, Bikini and Apolo as well. A huge, five-room nightclub, Razzmatazz is particularly good for spotting up-and-coming bands, which often play in the small upstairs bars.

In the past couple of years, a crackdown by the authorities has seen dozens of the Ciutat Vella's little live music bars close, and the city's scene is slightly poorer as a result. But, Sidecar has managed to survive, showing cult punk bands and arch new pop acts in its basement quarters off Plaça Reial.

Meanwhile, there's a resilient local jazz scene, with some atmospheric venues that welcome international talent but also have plenty of local regulars. In the Barri Gòtic there's Jamboree (p.164) and the Harlem Jazz Club, both of which have live acts almost every night, while other classics such as Luz de Gas and La Cova del Drac are towards Diagonal.

In the summer months, the festival calendar is even busier than usual, with a burgeoning series of rock, pop and dance festivals (see Essentials, p.34) as well as more local events, which often include free concerts. Also in the summer, venues across the city organise open-air concerts. Those at La Pedrera (p.92) and Parc de la Ciutadella (p.70) are particularly popular. Check www.bcn.cat for upcoming events.

Opera & Classical Music

The sumptuous Liceu (p.164) opera house remains the grande dame of the local opera and classical music scene. Extensively refurbished following a devastating blaze, it has little luxuries like English-language subtitles on the seat backs, as well as an impressive programme of in-house and visiting productions, some of which sell out months in advance. There are also frequent foyer recitals and children's events.

The fairy-tale building of the Palau de la Música (p.211) may be the main draw for most tourists, but there's also a full programme of symphonic concerts by regional orchestras. Concerts here can be rather staid, with few surprises or little-known composers. For something a little more challenging, head to the sleek, modern l'Auditori concert hall. It's home to the excellent Orquestra Simfònic de Barcelona and also hosts international orchestras and performers. There is also a series of modern music, symphonic classics, early music and world music concerts. It's worth keeping an eye out for concerts in the city's churches, particularly around Christmas and Easter; these are often free, and are held in some of the city's loveliest monuments, including Santa Maria del Mar (p.71).

Theatres

Gran Teatre del Liceu		
La Rambla	93 485 99 13	www.liceubarcelona.com
L'Auditori		
C/ Lepant	93 247 93 00	www.auditori.org
Palau de la Música		
C/Palau de la Música	93 295 72 00	www.palaumusica.org
Teatre Nacional de Catalunya		
Pl Arts, 1	93 306 57 00	www.tnc.es
Teatre Tivoli		
C/ Casp, 8-10	93 412 20 63	www.serviticket.com

Film

For such a photogenic city, it's astonishing that Barcelona doesn't show up more often on the silver screen. This is changing, though: much of *Perfume* was shot here, and in summer 2007 Woody Allen caused uproar by shutting off whole chunks of the Barri Gòtic and Born to shoot a film (untitled, at the time of writing) with Scarlett Johansson. Other productions are also in the pipeline.

While the city may not show up much on screen, film is big news in Barcelona: there's an array of film festivals, with everything from the huge Asian Film Festival (April to May, www.casaasia.es) to the quirky Mecal (September, www.mecalbcn.com), which shows 10 minute shorts. Visit www.bcn.cat for details of upcoming events.

In the summer months, there are also several outdoor cinemas that are good for picnics and languid evenings. Sala Montjuïc, in the castle at the hill's summit, screens a mix of recent releases and classics, many of which are shown in English with Spanish or Catalan subtitles (www.salamontjuic.com). The CCCB's Gandules season covers the Pati de les Dones with deckchairs and screens arthouse classics (www.cccb.org).

If it's blockbusters you're after, most cinemas in the city screen dubbed versions of films, but purists head to Cine Verdi, Renoir-Floridablanca, and the slightly more multiplex-like Yelmo Icària Cineplex. All show films in their original language, meaning you can actually watch English-language flicks in English (look for the VO sign next to the title).

Cinemas

Cine Verdi			
C/ Verdi, 32		93 238 79 90	www.cines-verdi.com
Renoir-Floridablanca			
C/ Floridablanca, 135		93 228 93 93	www.cinesrenoir.es
Yelmo Icària Cineplex			
C/ Salvador Espriu, 61		93 221 75 85	www.yelmocineplex.es

Liceu from the stage

Profile

Culture

If you're looking for flamenco and bullfighting you've come to the wrong place: Barcelona is uniquely Catalan.

Although it is firmly within the borders of Spain, many Barcelonins would describe themselves as Catalan rather than Spanish. The region's relationship with the Spanish crown has long been fraught and Catalan culture is a world away from stereotypical Spain, taking many visitors by surprise. Catalonia was an independent nation until the 18th century, and its language, cuisine and customs are jealously guarded to this day.

However, Barcelonins are also proud of the cosmopolitan, European feel to their capital, and the city is changing at a breakneck pace as it smartens up its ancient buildings and develops new business, tourism and retail zones.

People

Catalans have a reputation within Spain for being unapproachable and surly, but this is a tad unfair as once you get to know the locals you'll find that they're warm and loyal. They also have a reputation for being frugal (some might say tight-fisted) but this is most visible to foreigners in low levels of tipping, with around 2% to 3% considered perfectly reasonable.

Barcelona is a politically charged city, with a long history of communist, republican and anarchist political groups. It has retained an 'alternative', vaguely leftist feel, particularly in comparison to the more conservative, devout Spain of

the south. Today, that alternative spirit is more likely to be expressed through the arts than street protests.

Barcelona's cultural confidence stems from its medieval glory days as a seafaring, mercantile power. The Romans and Visigoths left their political and artistic mark before the city fell under the rule of the Spanish and French, which is more evident today. These days, the city is becoming increasingly cosmopolitan as Europeans, Africans and Latin Americans move here, attracted by the booming economy and easy-going lifestyle. Catalan society is progressive and tolerant.

Traditions

Many Catalan traditions have a certain daredevil appeal. Adrenaline-filled events such as castellers (human towers standing up to nine men tall, topped with a tiny child) and the correfoc (a raucous parade full of fireworks, dragons and devils) are emblematic of Catalan culture, and are enjoyed as much by the young as by the old.

The biggest dates on the Catalan calendar are Sant Jordi (April 23, p.36), Sant Joan (June 23) and the Festa de la Mercè (September, p.38), all these are celebrated with colourful, noisy parades and city-wide partying.

Food & Drink

Sat squarely between the Mediterranean and the rich farmland of inland Catalonia, Barcelona's cuisine blends the land and the sea with spectacular results. Cured meats, cheeses and seafood are outstanding, while the hearty sausages and stews of the region are profoundly satisfying.

One of these stews, *mar i muntanya* (sea and mountain) is said to represent the full Catalan landscape, containing both *mar* (seafood) and *muntanya* (meat).

Of course, this is still technically Spain, and tapas (a multitude of small dishes, to be shared) are available in many forms, everywhere from grubby, traditional little bars to gleaming haute cuisine restaurants.

The cheapest time to eat out is lunchtime. Most restaurants, whether traditional or international, offer a set meal (*menú del día*), which at €7 to €10 is often great value. Expect a starter, main course and dessert or coffee, as well as wine, water and bread, and the chance to try some signature Spanish dishes, such as gazpacho (cold tomato soup, heavy on the garlic). Paella, a spiced rice cooked with seafood, vegetables and often rabbit or chicken, is traditionally served on Thursdays, while other dishes seem to come and go as they please. Bacallà, salted cod, sounds revolting but can be sublime; the fish is soaked for days, yielding plump fillets with a delicate flavour.

Instead of buttering their bread, Catalans like to crush tomato into the dough and dribble olive oil and salt over it; sometimes they also rub garlic on it. This is known as *pa amb tomaquet* and is a local institution; the perfect accompaniment to jamón (dark, rich-flavoured cured ham).

Catalonia is gradually earning itself a foothold on the wine map: look for rich, heavy reds from Priorat, or whites and rosés from Costers del Segre and Empordà.

Eating out is affordable, a meal with wine can be managed for €25 a head, and there's a fantastic array of Catalan, Basque, traditional Spanish, French, Italian and fusion food. Kitchens don't generally get busy until 21:00, with 22:00 a far more normal time to meet for supper. Restaurants then stay open until the early hours. Many restaurants close on Mondays, and often for a couple of weeks in August. Catalans are very family orientated and restaurants tend to welcome children regardless of the time, although there are still many spots for business meetings or romantic suppers.

Although Catalan restaurants and tapas bars abound, there are also plenty of international restaurants serving everything from Nepali to Ethiopian cuisine. Many of these are still rather scruffy, but there's a growing brood of chi-chi Indian, Thai and fusion places opening up around town.

Religion

Nationally, 94% of the population claims to be Roman Catholic. However, going to church is generally left to the older generations and Latin Americans. There are sizeable Evangelist and Jehovah's Witness communities in Barcelona. Catalonia's large North African and Pakistani populations means that there is a growing Muslim community, with many Islamic centres (but no mosque).

The Church is most visible in Spain on religious holidays, when there are parades and special services. These include Christmas and Easter Week, and important Saints' days.

Politics

The Spanish government is a constitutional monarchy ruled by King Juan Carlos I, who became king at the end of Franco's reign. Currently, the party in power is the Socialist PSOE, with José Luis Rodríguez Zapatero as prime minister. National elections will be held in 2008.

However, it's easy to feel that all this is a world away from Barcelona. Spain is one of Europe's most devolved nations, and Catalonia has its own government, the Generalitat, which decides matters such as health, education and policing. The Generalitat is currently a socialist-led coalition, with Jose Montilla Aguilera as president.

Meanwhile the Ajuntament (city hall) is responsible for much of Barcelona's everyday operations, covering issues such as refuse collection. Relations between the Generalitat and Spanish government are often tense; and Catalonia has a small but vocal movement demanding independence for the region.

History

Roman outpost, mighty medieval port, hotbed of revolution: Barcelona has been many things over the centuries, but it's never been boring.

Foundation Of The City

Although tribes such as the Laetani originally inhabited the area, seafaring Carthaginians are believed to have founded Barcelona in around 230 BC.

Romans & Visigoths

When the Romans defeated the Carthaginians, they made a military camp of Mons Taber, today a maze of backstreets between Plaça Sant Jaume and Carrer Ample. Although overshadowed by nearby Tarraco (Tarragona), the capital of the province, Roman Barcino flourished as a market town, eventually establishing its own harbour and coin mint. In the fifth century, Rome crumbled under repeated onslaughts by Barbarian tribes and Barcelona was left to the mercy of the Visigoths, who crossed over the Pyrenees from Gaul. Under Theodoric the Great, the Visigoths (West Goths) united with the Ostrogoths (East Goths) and in 511 ruled most of the peninsula, with Barcelona as their capital.

Short-Lived Moorish Rule

The peninsula was invaded by the Moors in the early 700s. An Islamic dynasty, the Umayadds, replaced the Visigoths.

Barcelona was occupied, but not long enough to have absorbed any lasting impression of Moorish culture. It was liberated in 801 by Louis of Aquitaine, who used it as a buffer zone to protect France.

The Catalan Empire

Despite occasional attacks by Arab pirates and a sacking by Al-Mansur in 985, Barcelona's star was on the rise. Guifre El Pelòs, aka Wilfred the Hairy, was the first Barcelonin count to rule an independent Catalonia (878-897). Under Ramon Berenguer III (1082-1131), Catalonia expanded as far north as Nice in France, and Ibiza and Mallorca were captured from the Moors. Catalonia now had an empire, and Barcelona was its capital.

Catalonia was united with neighbouring Aragon in 1137, though each region controlled its own affairs. Under Jaume I (1213-76), Valencia was captured. Sardinia, Corsica, Naples, the Roussillon region of south-east France, and even Athens were soon added and trade flourished. Catalan merchants had exclusive rights to gold from Sudan, and Barcelona was a port to rival Venice and Genoa.

During this period the foundations of future democracy were laid. An early system of law, the Usatges de Barcelona, and a city council, the Consell de Cent, were founded. The origins of today's Generalitat can be traced back to a parliament formed in 1282. It was around this time that some of the major landmarks of today's Barri Gòtic sprang up, many of them incorporating old Roman remains. The Palau del Bisbe is one example; Gothic stained glass windows lead onto a Roman arcade. La Ribera's Palacio Berenguer d'Aguilar is another, and now houses the Picasso Museum (p.10).

Decline Of The Empire

In the 14th century, Barcelona's economy began to falter. The rising naval power of the Ottoman empire bankrupted the city in 1391. Meanwhile, neighbouring Castile was making astute alliances and growing rich on its wool and corn trade. Following the 1469 alliance with Aragon, Castile granted all overseas trade to Seville and Cadiz. Castile was entering its golden age, while Catalonia was in decline.

In an effort to challenge Castilian dominance, Catalonia signed the Pact of Ceret with the French in 1640. This made Catalonia a free republic under the protection of the French King, Louis XIII. In 1659 however, Barcelona was taken by Castilian troops under King John Joseph of Austria. Rosellò, Conflent, Vallespir and part of Cerdanya were annexed to the French.

During the Spanish War of Succession, Catalonia backed the wrong horse, supporting a British-Austrian alliance against the French Bourbon pretender, Felipe. The Austrian Habsburg claim dissolved, leaving Catalonia to defend itself against Felipe alone. After a year-long siege of Barcelona, Felipe's forces triumphed and Catalonia fell to Spain in 1714. Felipe then set about punishing a defenceless Barcelona.

After sacking the city, Felipe outlawed the Catalan language (by now largely spoken only by the peasantry), declared Catalonia a province of Spain and demolished a suburb of the city to make room for a huge fortress, the

The Arc de Triomf

Cuitadella, that watched over Barcelonins. Today it is the site of one of Barcelona's loveliest green areas, el Parc de la Ciutadella (p.70).

By the end of the 18th century, Barcelona's attentions turned towards industry and trade with Spain and the 'new world' across the Atlantic. One of the world's first textile dyeing factories was inaugurated in 1783, and provided 75,000 jobs for Barcelonin workers.

The Expansion

Thanks to its cotton industry, 19th century Barcelona enjoyed a revival and became the seat of an autonomous Catalan government. Between 1890 and 1915, the bourgeoisie, growing rich on a tide of industrial production and keen to maximise influence within Spain, financed an adventurous plan of urban growth beyond the old city walls.

Called L'Eixample (The Expansion), it was much-needed, as the old city was crowded and suffering from unhealthy living conditions.

Eixample became the playground for a generation of unusually gifted architects who pioneered the Modernisme movement. They included Lluís Domènech i Muntaner, Josep Puig i Cadafalch, Josep Maria Jujol and Antoni Gaudí. Barcelona's *renaixença*, or renaissance, also saw the resurrection of the Catalan language and the emergence of poets such as Jacint Verdaguer. Enric de Prat de la Riba, meanwhile, became the first president of the Commonwealth of Catalonia, comprising the provinces of Barcelona, Girona, Tarragona and Lleida.

The General Strike

Through the early 20th century, Barcelona endured similar troubles to other industrialising nations. Growing disparity in wealth and the competing philosophies of the political left and right began to create social rifts. These were exacerbated by Spain's economic problems during the Great War (1914-1918), which caused factories to close and mass unemployment.

The capitalist classes feared a Russian-style revolution and leaned heavily on workers' unions such as the CNT (Confederación Nacional de Trabajo), many of whose members were blacklisted or even assassinated. Anarchist unionist activity grew as a result, leading to the general strike of 1917, which ended in bitter riots and 33 deaths in Barcelona. Another general strike followed in 1919. The Primo de Rivera dictatorship (1923-30) banned all organisations and literature related to anarchism, which led anarchists to resort to ever more violent methods. Primo de Rivera, a monarchist, abolished the Catalan commonwealth in 1925. Curiously enough, he was a Catalan himself by birth.

Civil War & Franco

During the Civil War (1936-1939) Barcelona became the principle seat of Spain's Republican government, the Popular Front. But, perpetual squabbling between the different factions – socialist, communist and anarchist, plus the trade unions they were allied to – severely weakened the Republican defence. The Civil War ravaged the city, and the Republicans were defeated by General Francisco Franco's right-wing falangists, who were bolstered by German military support.

The President of the Generalitat, Lluís Companys, a supporter of the failed Republic, fled to France along with thousands of others. When Germany invaded France, the Gestapo delivered him back to Spain and he was executed. His last words, spoken in front of the firing squad, were 'visca (long live) Catalunya'.

Once in power, Franco set about 'reincorporating' Catalonia into Spain. This involved public burnings of Catalan literature, the outlawing of Catalan street names and banning the language's use in television, radio, print and the classroom. In 1944, there was an attempted coup by local communists, and throughout the 40s there were a series of bombings, shootings and assassinations. But these achieved little, and opponents of the regime turned to peaceful protests instead.

Barcelona Timeline

230BC	Carthaginians settle in the area
100BC	Roman camp of Mons Taber established
400-500	Visigoths invade
711	Barcelona occupied by Moors
801	Louis of Aquitaine and his Frankish forces liberate Barcelona
1162	Catalonia united with Aragon under Alfonso II
1213	Jaume I (The Conqueror) proclaimed King
1220s	Birth of Catalan Gothic style in Barcelona
1298	Construction of the Gothic cathedral begins
1385	Addition of the cloister of Santa Eulalia to the cathedral
1479	Marriage of the Catholic monarchs, Isabella and Fenando, unites Aragon and Castile
1847	Construction of Liceu Theatre begins
1852	Birth of the architect Antoni Gaudi
1873	Abdication of King Amadeo I and declaration of first Spanish Republic
1874	Restoration of Bourbon monarchy with Alfonso XII as king
1893	Birth of painter and sculptor Joan Miró
1899	Barcelona Football Club is founded
1904	Birth of surrealist painter Salvador Dali
1923	A Catalan, Primo de Rivera, becomes Spain's dictator

1929	Universal Exhibition comes to Barcelona. Poble Espanyol is built to host it
1929	Second Republic of Spain
1930	Catalonia declares autonomy
1936	Spanish Civil War begins
1939	Republican Barcelona falls. End of Spanish Civil War General Franco takes power
1953	Spain joins the United Nations
1975	Franco dies. Power passes to King Juan Carlos I
1977	Adolfo Suarez is elected President and grants Catalonia autonomy
1980	Jordi Puyol elected President of Barcelona's Generalitat
1992	FCBarcelona win their first European Champions Cup. Barcelona hosts the Olympic Games
1997	Joan Clos becomes Mayor
2003	Pascal Maragall replaces Jordi Pujol as President of the Generalitat
2004	Torre Agbar unveiled in Glòries as part of Poble Nou development
2006	FCBarcelona win their second European Cup. Jordi Hereu becomes mayor. José Montilla Aguilera is voted president

Barcelona Today

The past 20 years have seen Barcelona rise to become one of Europe's most exciting and dynamic cities.

After Franco

On 20 November 1975, General Francisco Franco died. Under the democratically elected government of Adolfo Suarez that followed, Catalonia was granted autonomy in 1977. The Catalan language was re-introduced to classrooms the following year. The Catalan Parliament held its first elections in 1980, and Jordi Pujol was elected as President of the Generalitat, holding office until 2003. During this time, as Catalonia modernised and opened itself to foreign markets, its economy, culture and language all flourished.

The New Catalan Empire

Barcelona is a model cosmopolitan city, attracting foreign investment and immigration from other EU countries. Its redevelopment schemes, many of which were in preparation for the Olympics, have been much praised. Its tourism industry, kickstarted by the Olympics, continues to thrive, and the city is a beacon of industrial design. Barcelona, now two millennia old, is in the middle of yet another *renaixença*.

Barcelona Overview

Jordi Pujol, the ex-President of the Generalitat, once likened Catalonia to a locomotive pulling the Spanish economy along

City skyline

without ever controlling its driver. Despite playing second fiddle to Madrid politically, Barcelona fulfils a vital role in Spain's economy, contributing almost 15% of its overall GDP. It has a large tertiary sector (tourism and services) that make up more than half of its local economy. There is a reliance on heavy industry (iron, steel, copper), and it is accumulating technology parks, such as the Barcelona Biomedical Research Park in Vila Olímpica. Another growth sector is the automobile industry; Volkswagen-owned Seat's opening of a new plant in the suburb of Martorell provided 12,000 local jobs, making around 450,000 cars a year.

New Developments

Once a dilapidated industrial ghost town, the district of Poble Nou is getting the kind of make-over its neighbour Vila Olímpica received in the run up to the Olympics. This ambitious scheme of regeneration is referred to as 22@ Barcelona, and aims to provide new housing, business and technical facilities to lure innovative companies and foreign investment. Its showpiece, the Jean Nouvel-designed Torre Agbar tower (often known locally as *el supositori*) was finished in 2004, but there is still a lot left to do in the rest of district. Since the project was approved in 2000, 300 firms have been drawn in and many more are expected to follow. It is hoped the development will eventually create over 130,000 jobs and increase Poble Nou's current 4% share in economic production to over 15%. It sounds rather optimistic, but then, so too did plans for the Olympics.

El Forum

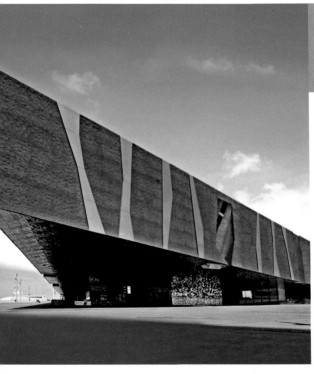

Fira de Barcelona

Continuing the commercial traditions of its golden age as a medieval port, the Catalan capital is a popular business location for the international market attracting more foreign investment than any other Spanish city. The impressive Fira de Barcelona congress centre in Plaça d'Espanya hosts five of the 11 top trade events in Europe, including the 3GSM mobile phone convention and Bread and Butter, an urban fashion fair. The centre's facilities are being extended in the Gran Via M2 development.

Tourism

Tourism accounts for a great deal of Barcelona's booming economy. In 1990 1.7 million tourists visited the city; by 2000 this figure had almost doubled and by 2005, it had passed five million. The city is especially popular for short stays, and was winner of the 2006 British Travel Award for Top Short Break Destination. New ferry terminals have also become popular for cruise liners. An extraordinary total of nine UNESCO World Heritage sites adds to the popular appeal. The Gaudí trail alone has seven, including La Sagrada Familia (p.96), his incredible unfinished church.

Barcelona's museums are popular, with the recently revamped Museu Picasso (p.71) and the innovative CosmoCaixa science museum (p.96) among the most visited. Tourisme de Barcelona reckons that the city's 'places of interest' receive more than 17 million visitors a year. The vibrant, chaotic nightlife is strong, and attracts Europe's young and trendy, while the Catalonian gastronomic scene lures in the gourmet crowd

Many visitors time their trip to coincide with big fiestas or music festivals. La Mercè (p.38) is by far the biggest, and for a few days the whole city can feel like one giant party.

Barcelona has also been busy making itself into an important business hub. It's the world's third most visited congress destination, with several historic venues. The newly unveiled CCIB international convention centre is capable of hosting up to 15,000 people. Business trips, conventions and fairs account for over half of all visitors.

Imaginative plans to increase tourism are still constantly being hatched. Most years are given a theme (such as Picasso, science, reading or design), which is used as a focus for exhibitions, workshops and events, and attracts many an eager tourist wishing to learn more. To cater for the ever-swelling tourist ranks, new hotels are opening all the time: by 2008 there should be some 30,000 hotel rooms available.

Population

Barcelona is Spain's second most populous city. In 1979, the population stood at a peak of almost two million. By 2000, it had slimmed down to around 1,500,000 after an exodus to nearby towns. In 2006, according to city council statistics, the population had risen again, to 1,605,602. This increase is attributed to the return of young people from the suburbs. There are more 30 to 34 year-olds (146,847) than any other age group.

By 2015, the population is expected to fall to around 1,590,700. Female residents outnumber males by 100,000. Male life expectancy is 77.5 years, while for women it's 84.3.

Maps

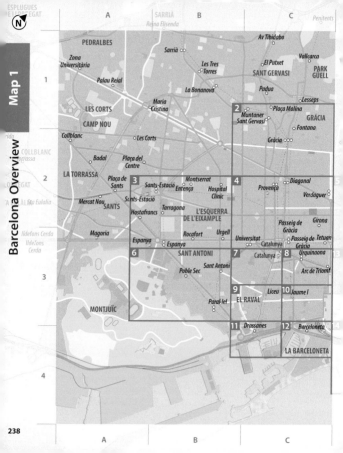

Map 1

Barcelona Overview

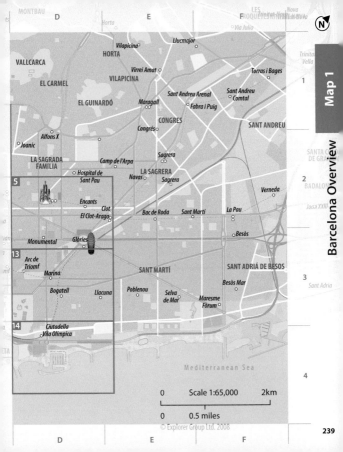

Map 1

MONTBAU

LES ROQUETES

Nova

Horta

Via Julia

VALLCARCA

Trinitat Vella

Vilapicina

Llucmajor

HORTA

EL CARMEL

Virrei Amat

VILAPICINA

Torras i Bages

1

EL GUINARDÓ

Maragall

Sant Andreu Arenal

Fabra i Puig

Sant Andreu Comtal

CONGRES

SANT ANDREU

Congrés

SANTA C
DE GRÀ

Alfons X

Sagrera

Joanic

LA SAGRADA
FAMILIA

Camp de l'Arpa

LA SAGRERA

BADALON

Navas

Sagrera

Hospital de
Sant Pau

2

5

Verneda

Encants

Joan XXIII

Clot

El Clot-Aragó

Bac de Roda

Sant Martí

La Pau

Monumental

Glòries

Besòs

13

Arc de
Triomf

Marina

SANT MARTÍ

SANT ADRIÀ DE BESÒS

Bogatell

Llacuna

Poblenou

Besòs Mar

Sant Adrià

Selva
de Mar

Maresme
Fòrum

3

14

Ciutadella
Vila Olímpica

TA

Mediterranean Sea

4

0   Scale 1:65,000   2km

0   0.5 miles

© Explorer Group Ltd. 2008

D   E   F

Legend

These maps include the most interesting bits of Barcelona. Museums, parks, beaches and shops are all marked, and the legend below explains what's what.

There are also coloured annotations dotted about the maps. These correspond to entries in four chapters of the book: Exploring, Going Out, Shopping and Sports & Spas. Anywhere with a green number, for example, will be from the Going Out chapter. It might be a cinema, bar, restaurant or club, but the review will be included in that chapter. The other colour codes are below.

00 Exploring   **00 Going Out**   **00 Shopping**   **00 Sports & Spas**

Legend

H Hotel/Resort	Land	Highway
血 Heritage/Museum	Pedestrian Area	Major Road
+ Hospital	Built up Area/Building	Secondary Road
Park/Garden	Industrial Area	Other Road
Agriculture	Water	)= = =(Tunnel
Shopping	Beach	Railway Station
Education	**†** Church	Cable Car
Stadium	**⊠** Post Office	Train (Renfe)
Boats	**ℹ** Tourist Info	Train (F.G.C.)
	RAVAL Area Name	**O** Metro
		⊕ International Airport

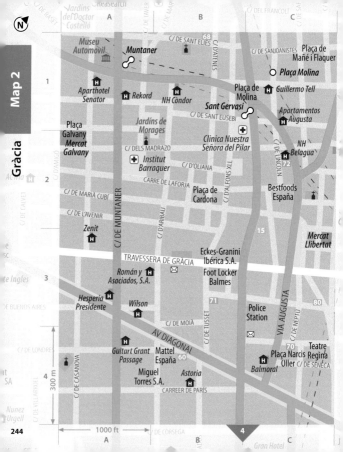

d'Elisard Sala.

C/ DEL PALAU

C/ DE ROBRENYO

A

B

City Park

C

Esc Univ. de
Professorat
D'E.G.B

Abba
Sants

Jardins
de Màlaga

Panasonic

C/ DE STA CATERINA

C/ DEL VALLESPIR

C/ D'ENRIC BARGES

Bus
Station

Sants-Estació

Barcelo-
Sants

Sants-Estació

Preso Model

Plaça de
Joan Peiró

Plaça
dels Països
Catalans

C/ DE PROVENÇA

C/ DE PRÈMIA

Esclat
Mallorca
Expo

Abbot

Parc de l'Espanya
Industrial

C/ DE MALLORCA

C/ DE WATT

Trades SA

Jardins
de Safo

H10 Itaca

C/ DE RECTOR TRIADÓ

C/ DE L'ELISI

C/ DE VILAMARÍ

C/ DEL SANT CRIST

Plaça d'Antoni
Pérez i Moya

Tarragona

St. Lorenzo

C/ DEL REI MARTÍ

Police
Station

Hostafrancs

C/ DE SANT NICOLAU

76

C/ DE TARRAGONA

C/ DEL MOIANÈS

C/ DE SANTS

Vincci Arena

C/ DEL CONSELL DE CENT

NH
Sant'Angelo

C/ DE GLÒRIA

Mercat
Hostafrancs

Parc
Joan Miró

Poliesportiu
Joan Miró

C/ DE L'ALIGA

C/ D'HOSTAFRANCS

C/ PRÍNCEP JORDI

San
Angel

C/ DE SANT ROC

Catalonia
Barcelona Plaza

C/ DE LLANÇÀ

Onix Fira

C/ DE LA CONSTITUCIÓ

Azul

Pl
Braus
Les Arenes

300 m

GRAN VIA DE LES CORTS CATALANES

Plaça
d'Espanya

Police
Station

AC Vilamari

Espanya

Espanya

1000 ft

Palau de la
Metal·lúrgia

6

A

B

C

Map 3

Eixample

C/ DE CÓRSEGA

Universitat
Industrial

Nuñez
Urgell

Hosp. Clínic
i Provincial

Plaça del
Ferrer i C

C/ D'ENTENÇA

Jardíns de
Montserrat

Entença Montserrat

Hospital
Clínic

Jardíns de
Marcia Merce
Marçal

Facultat de
Medicina

C/ DE PROVENÇA

C/ DE ROCAFORT

58

Catalonia
Roma

C/ DE VILADOMAT

Zenit
Borrell

C/ DEL COMTE BORRELL

C/ DEL COMTE

Mercat
del Ninot

Moscou
Sanchez S

C/ DE MALLORCA

2

Amister

NH
Master

C/ D'ENTENÇA

C/ DE VALÈNCIA

C/ DE CALÀBRIA

C/ DE VILADOMAT

AB
Viladomat

Century
Park

4

Plaça del
Gall

C/ D'ARAGO

L'ESQUERRA
DE L'EIXAMPLE

Acevi
Villarroel

Fujifilm
Espana SA

3

C/ DE ROCAFORT

C/ DE CALÀBRIA

C/ DE VILADOMAT

C/ DEL COMTE BORRELL

C/ DEL COMTE

C/ DE VILLARROEL

C/ DE LA DIPUTACIÓ

Villa
Emilia

HCC Open

Casa
Golferichs

St Josep
Oriol

Urgell Soho

Rocafort

GRAN VIA DE LES CORTS CATALANES

300 m

GRAN VIA DE LE

Caledon
Apsis
Splendic

1000 ft

SANT ANTONI

D   E   F

Advance

Map 4

Eixample

Perill

C/ DEL PERILL

2

C/ DE CÓRSEGA

PTGE CAPUTXINS

Plaça de
Joan Carles I

Diagonal 17

Casa Comalat

Casa
Quadras 63

C/ DE ROSSELLÓ

Catalonia
Córcega 1

Gallery 64
Casa 13 Hotel
Mila

Casa de les
Punxes

AV DIAGONAL

Omm

Actual

Verdaguer

Casa
Thomas

Clinic
Figarola Pera

C/ DE MALLORCA

Plaça Mossèn
Jacint
Verdaguer 2

Hotel Majestic

Hotel Clari's

C/ DEL BRUC

C/ DE VALÈNCIA

Paseo de
Gràcia

Condes de
Barcelona

Mercat
Concepció

987 Barcelona

Passeig de
Gràcia

Regente

Claris

PG DE SANT JOAN

Saleses

C/ D'ARAGO

5

Prestige

Servei
Estació Arago

Girona 56

Europark 3

AC Deplomàtic

Jardins
Carli

Iberia

C/ DE LA DIPUTACIÓ

Catalonia
Berna

Passeig de
Gràcia

PG DE GRÀCIA

C/ DE ROGER DE LLÚRIA

23

GRAN VIA DE LES CORTS CATALANES

Plaça de
Tetuan 4

GRAN VIA

Grahvia
Husa
Barcelona

Apsis Atrium
Palace

Petit
Palace BCN

Palace

Ritz
Barcelona

C/ DE BRUC

Tetuan

C/ DE BAILEN

8

1000 ft

300 m

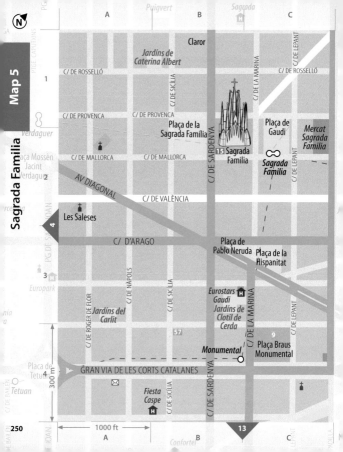

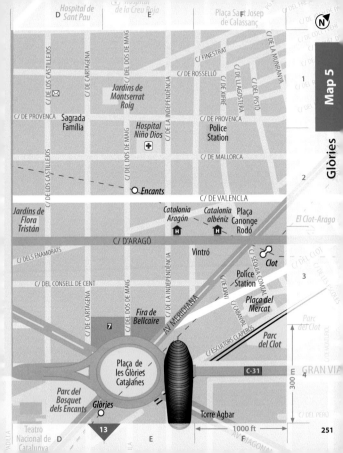

Map 6

Montjuïc

(N)

Espanya
Espa
C AC Vilamari

3

Palau de la
Metal·lúrgia

AV DEL PARAL·LEL

C/ NORD
C/ VALLS
C/ DELS M

Plaça de
l'Univers

Palau del
Cinquantenari

24 Pavelló
Mies Van
Der Rohe

GRABOS
19

Palau de
Congressos

C/ DE LLEIDA

Plaça de
carles
Buïgas

AV DE RIUS I TAULET

Capella
Romànica

La Font
Màgica

20

C/ DE LA FONT HONRADA

7

Palau de
Victòria Eugènia

Pl del
Marquès de
Foronda

Palau
d'italia

Prefectura
de Trànsit

H
Fira
Palace

Institut
Botànic

Pld e les
Cascades

Palau
d'Alfons XIII

Palau
d'Esports

AV DE LA TECNICA

Teater
Mercat
de les Flors

MIRADOR DEL PALAU NACIONAL

Institut
del Teater

1

22

Palau de les
Arts Grafiques

Teatre
Lliure

Palau Nacional
Museu D'Art
De Catalunya

Museu
Etnològic

Museu
Arqueològic

PTGE DE MARTRAS

C/ DE JUJIA

23

Jardins
d'Aclimatació

Palauet
Albèniz

Jardins de
joan Maragall

Teatre
Grec

Plaça de
Nemesi
Ponsati

Jardíns
de Laribal
Jardins
de Laribal

Fundació
Joan Miró

AV DE L'ESTADI

Plaça de
Neptu

Estadi Olímpic

PG OLIMPIC

AV DE MIRAMAR

Fundació 21
Joan Miró

C/ DELS TRES PINS

+

+

Estació
Parc Montjuïc

300 m

1000 ft

252

A

B

C

TRES PINS

Jardí de

Jardinsde

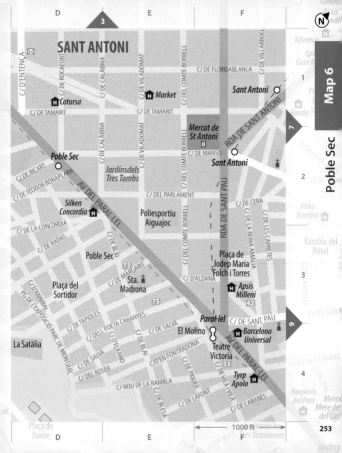

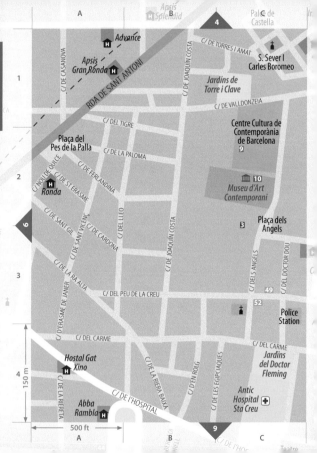

Map 7

Raval

Ⓝ

A   B   C

Apsis
Splendid

Palau de
Castella

4

C/ DE TORRES I AMAT

Advance

Apsis
Gran Ronda

RDA DE SANT ANTONI

C/ DE CASANOVA

C/ DE JOAQUIN COSTA

S. Sever I
Carles Boromeo

Jardins de
Torre i Clave

C/ DE VALLDONZEIA

1

C/ DEL TIGRE

Centre Cultura de
Contemporània
de Barcelona
9

Plaça del
Pes de la Palla

C/ DE LA PALOMA

C/ NOU DE LA DULCE

C/ DE ST ERASME

C/ DE FERLANDINA

🏛 **10**
Museu d'Art
Contemporani

Ronda

6

C/ DE SANT GIL

C/ DE SANT VICENC

C/ DE CARDONA

C/ DE LLEO

C/ DE JOAQUIN COSTA

Plaça dels
Angels
3

2

C/ DE LA RA ALTA

C/ DELS ANGELS

C/ DEL DOCTOR DOU

3

C/ D'ERASME DE JANER

C/ DEL PEU DE LA CREU

49

✝ **52**

Police
Station

C/ DEL CARME

C/ DEL CARME

Hostal Gat
Xino

Jardins
del Doctor
Fleming

4

150 m

C/ DE LA RIERETA

C/ DE LA RIERA BAIXA

C/ D'EN ROIG

C/ DE L'HOSPITAL

C/ DE LES EGIPCIAQUES

Antic
Hospital
Sta Creu ✚

Abba
Rambla

500 ft

A   B   C

9

Map 7

La Rambla

Inglaterra

Reding

Atlantis

Catalonia
Ramblas

Best Western
Hotel Regina

Duques de
Bergara

H10
Catalunya

Catalunya

Pulitzer

Plaça de
Catalunya

C/ DES TALLERS

C/ DE JOVELLANOS

C/ DE BERGARA

C/ DE PELAI

PG DE GRACIA

C/ FONTANELLA

Olivia Plaza

C/ DE LES RAMELLERES

Plaça de Vicenç
Martorell

Sta Anna

Continental

Plaça Ramon
Amadeu

C/ DE SANTA ANNA

Casa
Camper

C/ D'ELISABETS

Plaça del
Bonsucces

Royal
Poliorama

Olivia
Plaza

C/ DEL PINTOR FORTUNY

C/ DE XUCLA

Le Meridien
Barcelona

Riyoll
Rambla

C/ DE BERTRELLANS

Catalonia
Albinoni

Ambassador Turin

Hotel 1898

Montecarlo

Plaça de la Vila
de Madrid

Duc de la
Victoria

C/ DE LA MONISIO

LA RAMBLA

Betlem

C/ EN BOT

C/ DE LA VICTORIA

C/ DEL JERUSALEM

C/ DE PORTAFERRISSA

Plaça de
Cucurulla

Barcelona
Catedral

C/ D'EN ROCA

C/ DE DUC DE LA VICTORIA

C/ DELS BOTERS

Mercat de
la Boqueria

H10 Raca
del Pí

St Felip

Palau del

Plaça Nova

150 m

500 ft

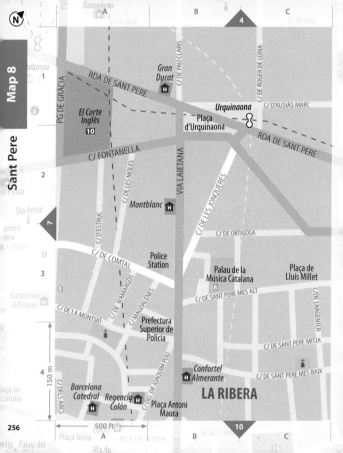

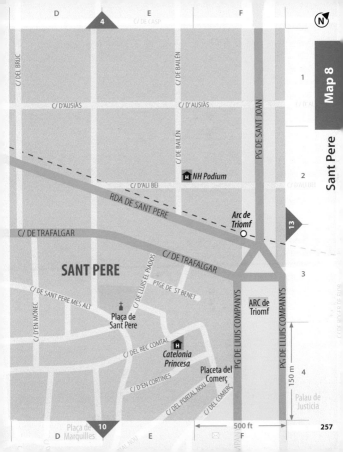

Map 8

Sant Pere

N

D · E · F

4

C/ DE CASP

1

C/ DEL BRUC

C/ D'AUSIÀS

C/ D'AUSIÀS

C/ DE BAILÉN

C/ DE BAILÉN

PG DE SANT JOAN

2

NH Podium

C/ D'ALI BEI

RDA DE SANT PERE

Arc de
Triomf

13

C/ DE TRAFALGAR

C/ DE TRAFALGAR

3

SANT PERE

C/ DE SANT PERE MES ALT

C/ D'EN MONEC

C/ DE LLUIS EL PIADOS

PTGE DE ST BENET

Plaça de
Sant Pere

C/ DEL REC COMTAL

PG DE LLUIS COMPANYS

ARC de
Triomf

Catelonia
Princesa

PG DE LLUIS COMPANYS

Placeta del
Comerç

C/ D'EN CORTINES

4

150 m

C/ DEL PORTAL NOU

C/ DEL COMERÇ

Palau de
Justicia

Plaça de
Marquilles

10

D · E · F

500 ft

257

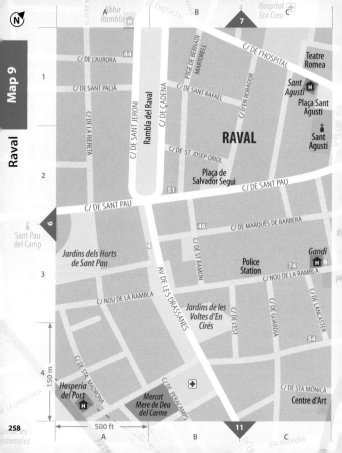

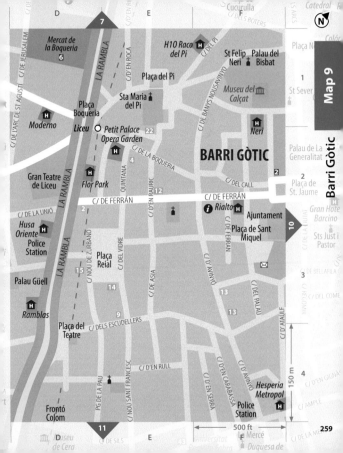

Map 9

Barri Gòtic

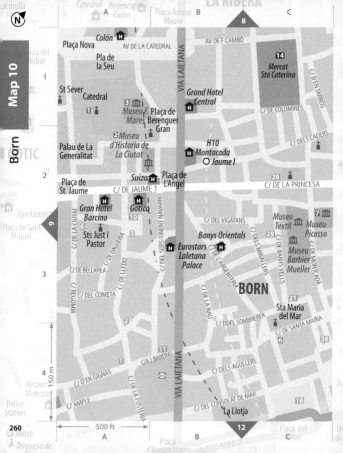

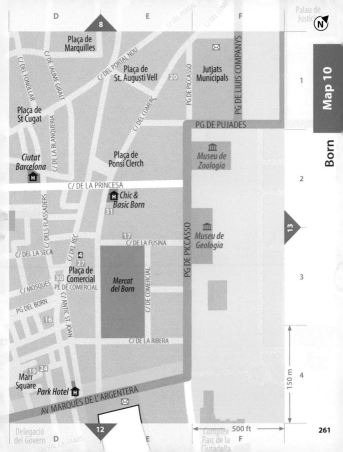

Map 10

Born

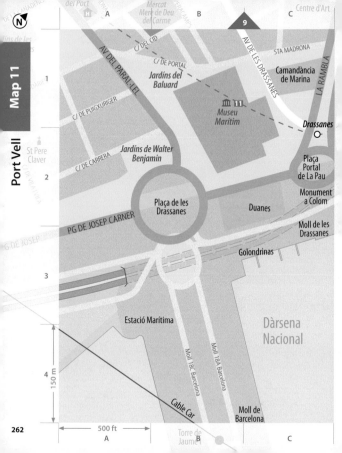

Map 11

Port Vell

del Port

A

B

Centre d'Art

C

9

CANADERS

STA MADRONA

CJ DEL CID

Mercat
Mere de Deu
del Carme

AV DE LES DRASSANES

LA RAMBLA

CJ DE PORTAL

Camandància
de Marina

AV DEL PARAL·LEL

**Jardíns del
Baluard**

1

CJ DE PUIGXURIGER

🏛 **11**
*Museu
Marítim*

Drassanes
○

**Jardíns de Walter
Benjamin**

St Pere
Claver

CJ DE CARRERA

Plaça
Portal
de La Pau

2

Monument
a Colom

**Plaça de les
Drassanes**

Duanes

Moll de les
Drassanes

PG DE JOSEP CARNER

PG DE JOSEP

Golondrinas

3

Estació Marítima

**Dàrsena
Nacional**

150 m

4

Moll 18C Barcelona

Moll 18A Barcelona

Cable Car

Moll de
Barcelona

500 ft

A

B

C

Torre de
Jaume I

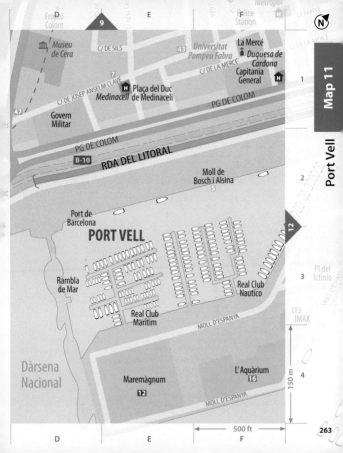

Map 11

Port Vell

Metropol

Police
Station

Frc/Rio
Colom

D

9

E

N

Museu
de Cera

C/ DE SILS

43

Universitat
Pompeu Fabra

La Mercé

Duquesa de
Cardona

C/ DE LA MERCÉ

Capitania
General

H

1

7

C/ DE JOSEP ANSELM CLAVÉ

H Plaça del Duc
Medinacell de Medinaceli

47

Govern
Militar

PG DE COLOM

B-10

PG DE COLOM

RDA DEL LITORAL

Moll de
Bosch i Alsina

5

2

Port de
Barcelona

12

PORT VELL

Rambla
de Mar

Real Club
Nautico

Pl del
Ictinio

3

Real Club
Maritim

MOLL D'ESPANYA

12

IMAX

Dàrsena
Nacional

Maremàgnum

12

L'Aquàrium

16

150 m

4

MOLL D'ESPANYA

500 ft

D

E

F

Map 12

Barceloneta

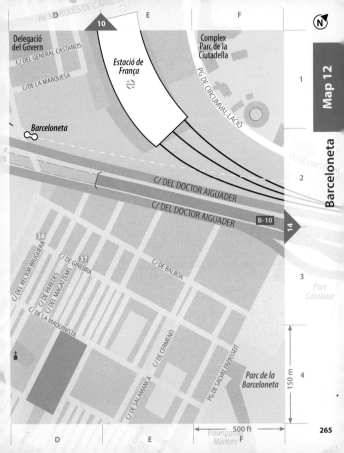

Map 12

N

AV M**D**RQUES DE L'ARGE

E

F

10

Delegació
del Govern

C/ DEL GENERAL CASTAÑOS

C/ DE LA MARQUESA

Estació de
França

Complex
Parc de la
Ciutadella

PG DE CIRCUMVAL·LACIÓ

1

Barceloneta

PG DE CIRCUMVA

C/ DEL DOCTOR AIGUADER

2

C/ DEL DOCTOR AIGUADER

B-10

14

38

C/ DEL RECTOR BRUGUERA

37

C/ DE GINEBRA

C/ DE PAREDES

C/ DEL MAGALLEMS

C/ DE LA MAQUINISTA

C/ DE BALBOA

Parc
Catalana

3

C/ DE CERMEÑO

C/ DE SALAMANCA

PG DE SALVAT PAPASSEIT

Parc de la
Barceloneta

150 m

4

500 ft

Poliesportiu
Marítim

D

E

F

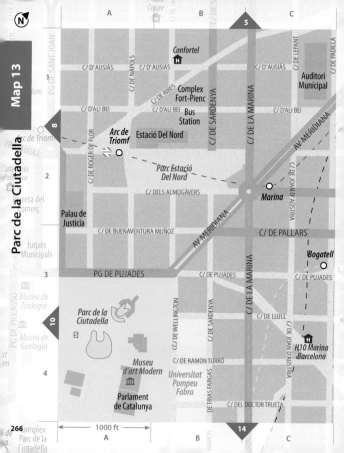

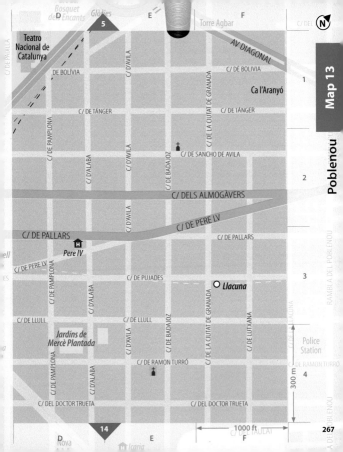

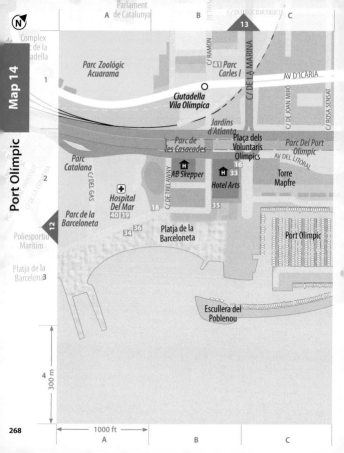

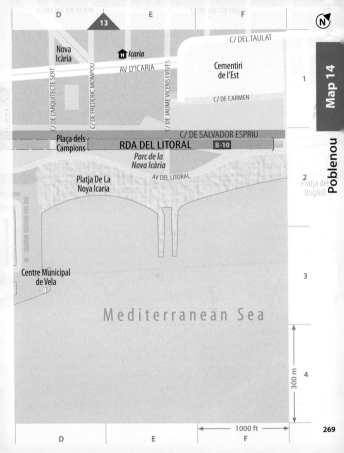

Map 14

Poblenou

C/ DEL DOCTOR TRUETA

D E F

C/ DEL DOCTOR TRUETA

13

N

C/ DEL TAULAT

Nova
Icària

Icaria

Cementiri
de l'Est

AV D'ICARIA

C/ DE CARMEN

C/ DE L'ARQUITECTE SERT

C/ DE FREDERIC MOMPOU

C/ DE JAUME VICENS I VIVES

C/ DE ROSA SENSAT

1

C/ DE SALVADOR ESPRIU

Plaça dels
Campions

RDA DEL LITORAL B-10

Parc de la
Nova Icària

Platja De La
Noya Icaria

AV DEL LITORAL

2

Platja del
Bogtell

Centre Municipal
de Vela

8

3

Mediterranean Sea

300 m

4

D E F

1000 ft

Explorer
Products

Residents' Guides

All you need
to know about
living, working
and enjoying life
in these exciting
destinations

Coming in 2008/9: Bangkok, Brussels, Mexico City, Moscow,
San Francisco, Saudi Arabia and Taipei

Mini Guides

Perfect pocket-sized
visitors' guides

Coming in 2008/9: Bangkok, Brussels, Mexico City, Moscow, San Francisco and Taipei

Activity Guides

Drive, trek, dive and swim... life will never be boring again

Check out www.explorerpublishing.com/products

Mini Maps

Fit the city in your pocket

Coming in 2008/9: Ajman, Al Ain, Bangkok, Brussels, Fujairah, Mexico City, Moscow, Ras Al Khaimah, San Francisco, Taipei, Umm Al Quwain

Maps

Wherever you are, never get lost again

Photography Books

Beautiful cities caught through the lens

Lifestyle Products & Calendars

The perfect accessories for a buzzing lifestyle

Check out www.explorerpublishing.com/products

Explorer Team

Publishing
Publisher Alistair MacKenzie
Associate Publisher Claire England
Assistant to Associate Publisher
Kathryn Calderon

Editorial
Group Editor Jane Roberts
Lead Editors David Quinn, Katie Drynan
Matt Farquharson, Sean Kearns,
Tim Binks, Tom Jordan
Deputy Editors Helen Spearman, Jakob
Marsico, Pamela Afram, Richard Greig,
Tracy Fitzgerald
Senior Editorial Assistant
Mimi Stankova
Editorial Assistants Grace Carnay,
Ingrid Cupido

Design
Creative Director Pete Maloney
Art Director Ieyad Charaf
Design Manager Alex Jeffries
Senior Designer Iain Young
Junior Designer Jessy Perera
Layout Manager Jayde Fernandes
Designers Hashim Moideen, Rafi Pullat,
Shawn Jackson Zuzarte
Cartography Manager
Zainudheen Madathil
Cartographers Juby Jose,
Noushad Madathil, Sunita Lakhiani
Traffic Manager Maricar Ong
Production Coordinator Joy Tubog

Photography
Photography Manager Pamela Grist
Photographer Victor Romero
Image Editor Henry Hilos

Sales & Marketing
Media Sales Area Managers
Laura Zuffa, Stephen Jones
Corporate Sales Executive Ben Merrett
Marketing Manager Kate Fox
Marketing Executive Annabel Clough
Marketing Assistant Shedan Ebona
Digital Content Manager
Derrick Pereira
International Retail Sales Manager
Ivan Rodrigues
Retail Sales Coordinators
Kiran Melwani, Sobia Gulzad
Retail Sales Supervisor Mathew Samuel
Retail Sales Merchandisers
Johny Mathew, Shan Kumar
Sales & Marketing Coordinator
Lennie Mangalino
Distribution Executives
Ahmed Mainodin, Firos Khan
Warehouse Assistant Najumudeen K.I.
Drivers Mohammed Sameer,
Shabsir Madathil

Finance & Administration
Finance Manager Michael Samuel
HR & Administration Manager
Andrea Fust
Admin Manager Shyrell Tamayo
Junior Accountant Cherry Enriquez
Accounts Assistant Darwin Lovitos
Administrators
Enrico Maullon, Kelly Tesoro
Driver Rafi Jamal, Mannie Lugtu

IT
IT Administrator Ajay Krishnan
Senior Software Engineer
Bahrudeen Abdul
Software Engineer Roshni Ahuja

Contact Us

▶ Reader Response
If you have any comments and suggestions, fill out
our online reader response form and you could win prizes.
Log on to **www.explorerpublishing.com**

▶ Newsletter
If you would like to receive the Explorer newsletter packed with
special offers, latest books updates and community news please
send an email to **Marketing@explorerpublishing.com**

▶ General Enquiries
We'd love to hear your thoughts and answer any questions
you have about this book or any other Explorer product.
Contact us at **Info@explorerpublishing.com**

▶ Careers
If you fancy yourself as an Explorer, send your CV (stating the
position you're interested in) to **Jobs@explorerpublishing.com**

▶ Designlab and Contract Publishing
For enquiries about Explorer's Contract Publishing arm and
design services contact **Designlab@explorerpublishing.com**

▶ Maps
For cartography enquries, including orders and comments,
contact **Maps@explorerpublishing.com**

▶ Corporate Sales
For bulk sales and customisation options, for this book or any
Explorer product, contact **Sales@explorerpublishing.com**